A Shorter Shīrazād

101 poems of Michael Field

For all those who love the magic and discipline of the old, authentic poetry

And for the new generations who have been deprived of their birthright of language and conjuration for so long

A Shorter Shīrazād

101 poems of Michael Field

Chosen, annotated, but *not* edited
by Ivor C Treby

First published in 1999 by De Blackland Press
World copyright © Ivor C Treby 1999

The right of Ivor C Treby to be identified as the author
of this work has been asserted by him in accordance
with the Copyright, Designs and Patents Act, 1988

A CIP catalogue record for this book
is available from the British Library.

ISBN 0-907404-05-7

Typeset by De Blackland Press
Printed on White Woodfree Bookwove and bound in Great Britain by
St Edmundsbury Press, Bury St Edmunds, Suffolk   250 copies only

Acknowledgements

This present book is the first section of two, of a planned selection of some 200 Michael Field poems under the collective title IN LEASH TO THE STRANGER; it is to be hoped that the 21st Century will not have begun before the whole project is at last completed.

Thomas Sturge Moore was the literary executor appointed by Michael Field, a thankless and particularly onerous task which he fulfilled with an enthusiasm and punctiliousness that lesser mortals might envy; in this he repaid with interest the friendship and concerned regard for his own literary work bestowed on him, in turn, by the two ladies whilst they were still alive. I am grateful to the current copyright holders, Leonie Sturge-Moore and Charmian O'Neil, for authorising this first publication of thirty three Michael Field poems, amongst others, as well as the quotation of excerpts from the voluminous Michael Field papers and the relevant correspondence of Thomas Sturge Moore and his family.

I am also indebted to the Keeper of Western Manuscripts at the Bodleian Library, University of Oxford, and to the Curator of Modern Literary Manuscripts at the British Library, for permission to quote from the papers in their charge, and for allowing me access to the texts of the unpublished poems.

My ambition to draw on all surviving sources of Michael Field autographs would have been unachievable without the co-operation, kindness, and patience of Bede Bailey (Blackfriars Archive) and Francis Collins (custodian of the Fortey Cache manuscripts). To them both, as ever, much thanks.

I extend heartfelt apologies to any copyright holders whose rights have unwittingly been infringed (in particular to the heirs and assignees of Charles Haslewood Shannon for the reproduction of his pastel portrait of Henry). Every effort has been made to trace all such, but without success.

Ivor C Treby   London, July 1999

Front cover: Katharine Harris Bradley (1846-1914) with Whym Chow (1897-1906), around 1903.

From light L17 in The MICHAEL FIELD Catalogue, itself taken from the photograph *(YCA— BUN Hlc 3)* kindly made available by the Archivist of Bristol University Library.

Back cover: Edith Emma Cooper (1862-1913), portrait head nearly in profile to left, May 1901. By Charles Haslewood Shannon: black and red chalk, touched with white, on reddish-brown paper, 12½" x 8½".

Bequeathed by Katharine Harris Bradley to The Birmingham Museums and Art Gallery *(246'14),* and here reproduced by kind permission of the Curator, Art Department: Paintings and Sculpture.

References

The following abbreviations have been used in the notes:

H   - prose in hand of Edith Cooper   M - prose in hand of Katharine Bradley
aka - also known as   cf - compare with   ob - died   pe - preface
rt - related to   s - stanza   sa - see also   v - verse   v.i. - see below

Other citations are 3-letter codes (such as WDH, SMF, JAM, OCS, YSA, ZJP). These include some of the published works of Michael Field:

DDD -	Dedicated	George Bell & Sons	London 1914
LAG -	Long Ago	George Bell & Sons	London 1889
MCT -	Mystic Trees	Eveleigh Nash	London 1913
PAD -	Poems of Adoration	Sands & Co.	London 1912
SAS -	Sight and Song	Elkin Mathews	London 1892
SMF -	A Selection, Poems of Michael Field	Poetry Bookshop	London 1923
TWF -	The Wattlefold	Basil Blackwell	Oxford 1930
UTB,C -	Underneath the Bough (two editions)	George Bell & Sons	London 1893
UTD -	Underneath the Bough	Mosher	Portland ME 1898
WAD -	Works and Days	John Murray	London 1933
WCF -	Whym Chow Flame of Love	Eragny Press	London 1914
WDH -	Wild Honey from various thyme	Fisher Unwin	London 1908
XBU -	Brutus Ultor	George Bell & Sons	London 1886
XNB -	Noontide Branches	Henry Daniel	Oxford 1899
XTM -	The Tragic Mary	George Bell & Sons	London 1890

And also:

FAL - Victorian Women Poets by Angela Leighton   Harvester Wheatsheaf 1992
FCR - Michael Field by Charles Ricketts   Tragara Press 1976
FES - Reminiscences of My Life by Elizabeth Sturge   1928
FLS - Reperusals and Re-collections by Pearsall Smith   Constable & Co 1936
FMS - Michael Field by Mary Sturgeon   Harrap & Co London 1922
JCM - Carmina #8, The Poetry of Michael Field by Edwin Essex   1931
VCR - Letters to "Michael Field" from Ricketts (1903-13)   Tragara Press 1981
VSW -Sappho: A Memoir and Translation by H.T. Wharton   Stott London 1885

Few of the above books are readily available in libraries. Codes beginning with a J relate to newspapers and magazines. Those beginning with an O or a Z indicate manuscripts only accessible in the collections of the Bodleian Library at Oxford, or of the British Library in London; Y codes signify manuscripts or similar material in other collections. For all these latter a reader's card is unavoidable, so it seems inappropriate to burden this text with shelfmarks when the MSS. would not, in any case, be available to the general uncertificated reader. However, such shelf marks (and details of the people referred to in the notes as well as fuller information on the lives and work of the two ladies) are fully documented in the key reference work:

MFC - The MICHAEL FIELD Catalogue a book of lists De Blackland Press 1998

This book also lists in chronological order by T number (such as T1645) some 1725 poems presently attributed to Michael Field.

Contents

Introduction

I The Poets

In May 1884 there was a household at Stoke Green, Bristol, which to all outward appearances was typically middleclass. It consisted of a married couple, James and Emma Cooper, their two daughters Edith and Amy, and Katharine Bradley, Emma's younger sister; to which one may probably add a couple of servants. Katharine and their widowed mother had originally lived with Emma and her husband in Kenilworth some 23 years previously, and it was here that the two girls were born, in 1862 and 1863; shortly after this Emma's health deteriorated, and her mother died. Katharine was then 21 and most of her time seems to have been spent looking after the two little girls; she was particularly devoted to the elder, Edith, who was just six years old. For a time this pattern had seemed set to change. Just after the death of her mother, Katharine became fleetingly entangled with, perhaps engaged to, a French sculptor turned stained glass artist; but he was to die suddenly, less than a month after they first met. The family moved several times, to Newton Leys in Derbyshire, then Solihull, then south to Bath, and eventually to Bristol.

Katharine had from a child shown a deep love of the classics and a natural talent for writing little poems, and her enthusiasms seem to have kindled a spark in Edith, who also began writing exotic plays when she was twelve. This fundamental division— Katharine for poetry and Edith for drama— set a pattern of interests which never substantially changed. In 1875 Katharine's first book of poetry THE NEW MINNESINGER was published by Longmans under the pseudonym 'Arran Leigh', and in 1881 she and her niece collaborated as 'Arran and Isla Leigh' on a second volume of drama and verse BELLEROPHÔN.

But May 1884 was pivotal, the month which saw the publication of their first major triumph, CALLIRRHOË / FAIR ROSAMUND, two separate plays bound together under yet another pseudonym, 'Michael Field'. This was a wise move, as a masculine name ensured their work would receive serious critical attention. And it succeeded beyond all reasonable expectation, attracting the enthusiastic praise of no less a poet than the aging

Robert Browning. The publication of H.T. Wharton's *Sappho* in 1885, containing the surviving fragments of that earlier poet's work, was to be the stimulus for LONG AGO (1889), "one of the most exquisite lyrical productions of the latter half of the nineteenth century"— so wrote John Miller Gray in *The Academy*. Browning had willingly overseen this work of his "two dear, Greek women" and his death that December was a great blow. (One wonders if he had lived to see UNDERNEATH THE BOUGH (1893) with its quotation from Fitzgerald's rendering of Khayyám's *Rubáiyát*, whether he might have tried to persuade them to change the title; that same 1889 he had been famously enraged at reading Fitzgerald's slight on his dead wife.) From then on the die was cast; the rest of their lives they devoted to their high art, Katharine as 'Michael' and Edith as 'Field', although they always insisted that they functioned as a single artistic unit.

There was to be one final bizarre tweak to their artistic domino in August 1891, when Edith nearly died of scarlet fever on their visit to Dresden. Because of a dangerously high temperature, her hair was cut as short as a boy's, and the nurse subsequently referred to her as 'Heinrich'. In its anglicised form this nickname stuck, and Edith, although still 'Field', became commonly referred to as 'Henry' from that time on until her death in 1913.

It is with the major span of their creative lives, 1884-1912, that this preliminary selection from the poetry of Michael Field is concerned.

II The Poetry

The notes reveal an apparent disproportion in contribution by the two writers, Michael's share is the larger. The reason, as hinted earlier on, is fairly straightforward: she wrote far more poetry than her niece. Yet this is an oversimplification; they "weeded each other's garden" (ZCC 213r), and there is scarcely a poem of Michael's that has not been 'passed' (ie proof-read), if not edited, by Henry. And the reverse was also true. Not all the poems are perfect; they wrote far too much. But in fairness, a lot of it was only for their eyes, and the unpublished work included in this anthology should be read with this in mind. And it is in this very unpubulished work that one can discover new facets of a fascinating personality, the "double-headed" nightingale (FLS 86). That happy handful of people who are already familiar with the

13

work of Michael Field will be dismayed at what is absent: where are *The Cliff, Love's unreason, 'Tiresias', La Gioconda, Unbosoming, Stream and Pool, Constancy, The Mummy invokes his Soul, The Forest, Old Ivories, A Flaw, Jason, Aridity*— above all, *Herself, 'Prologue', Fellowship* and *Fading* ? Some of these are excluded by virtue of the date restrictions, others to allow a wider variety; all are available elsewhere, and will in any case hopefully feature in the planned sequel collection. Meanwhile, rejoice in the rarely seen, and also in the largely unknown, pieces that *are* included: Henry conjuring up a train of Bacchantes, her haunted childhood, and a bloodthirsty Pharaonic princess; Michael getting sunburnt on a beach, eavesdropping in Perugia, and changing eyes with a Punch-and-Judy man's dog in a street of Victorian London. The unpublished pieces have been printed exactly as they stand in manuscript draft, with incomplete punctuation, and some words such as *and, could, which, would* abbreviated to *&, cd, wh, wd*; these have deliberately been left unedited to remind the reader that the received text is not necessarily in its finalised state.

III The Notes

I make no apology for the expository nature of the footnotes; syntax and vocabulary alike, as well as allusion, can be knotty and occasionally baffling. For several generations now the great classical myths and adventures have been rubbished away as irrelevant (the one exception seems to be if the myths originated in those annexed lands still ludicrously described as "holy"). References to the Maenads, and other ladies who lynch, are better enjoyed when one appreciates the connotations. Equally important can be an awareness of the circumstances in which a particular piece was written. Without this background detail, even comparatively well-known Michael Field poems such as T0446, T0489, T0824— and especially T0678, T0986 and T1287— are still subject to fantasy and crucial misinterpretation.

The reader is, of course, free to use or ignore these notes as he or she pleases; they are intended to help, rather than oppress. Not everyone needs, or appreciates, *ciceroni*. The source document citations are there only for those seeking confirmation of fact or the basis of a stated opinion; or simply for new enthusiasts (one hopes there may be many of these) eager and curious to know more. Major references have been listed separately. The

14

Journal, WORKS AND DAYS, running almost without interruption from 1888 to 1914 (ZJB through ZKF) and abstracted in WAD, is an engrossing record of the daily life of Michael Field.

IV New generations

"For some years my work has been done for 'the younger generation'— not yet knocking at the door, but awaited with welcome". So Michael Field, matter-of-factly, in his introduction to the American version of UNDERNEATH THE BOUGH (1898).

It is the received doctrine nowadays that *anyone* can write "poetry"; it comes off a shelf at the hypermarket, the product of an interactive chatter-culture in which everyone is talking and no-one is listening. All these babblers sound alike. It is impossible not to recognise the voice of Michael Field. He loved language, he knew his craft, he almost always had something interesting to say, and an arresting way to say it. He was never dull. Above all, he had HEART. His magic can still move us, uplift the spirit and illuminate the understanding with a sudden brilliant image, reach out to our common humanity. Some of the poems are not easy, but fresh minds relish challenge: why else the contemporary fascination with computer games?

Since his time rhyme and metre have been dismissed as trivial, elitist, namby-pamby. Hence the current deluge of formless, gormless and— most unforgivable of all— breathtakingly *boring* demospeak, delivered in the obligatory (and condescending) "poet's mumble". Can it be any surprise that poetry is now considered not even effete, merely jejune; that a recent *Spectator* called for 'A Hearse for British Verse' ? (JSP 05 June 1999)

The patient may yet recover. *Of course* one is not arguing for the archaic, and doggerel; for mangled syntax and the galumphing end-stopped rhyme, for po-faced rum-te-tum. Poetry will die if kept in a museum; but it must surely look to its roots, remember the structural *purpose* of metre and trope, its original functions to record and instruct, entertain and *engage*. It is in particular therefore to nimble young minds, as Michael Field himself would have wished, that these poems are offered: as open windows to the exciting world of ideas, ideals, language and myth.

Ivor C Treby   London   September 1999

Michael to Nature for his lady

I

O hoard the sunsets for her sake,
  Forbid the water-lilies break;
His sheaves the reaper shall not make
    Though wheat be golden,
Ere she, whose thirst thou lov'st to slake,
  Sweet Nature hath beholden.

II

The umbrage of Life's honey-tree
  Would bring me no felicity,
Till I the healing leaves should see
  Pressing her palms' sweet hollow;
New earth, new Heaven alike wd be
  Unveiled till she should follow.

III

And should she earliest reach the seat
  Nature, of thy perfection,
I could not find the country sweet:
  The simple tracking of her feet
All other rapture would defeat
  In recollection.

T0240   Four autographs are known, all but one (OYF 67o) in Katharine's hand.
The three others are all dated August 1884, with the additional footnote
Alum Bay (ICT: Isle of Wight). This text is that of OVC 34-5. The OPZ
autograph is of particular interest in that it immediately follows one of Katharine's
short prose pieces 'A Sunset' (OPZ 2a); which may have suggested the lyric itself.

his lady: It was about this time that Katharine became 'Michael', and here she is
        in a favourite courtly mode as Edith's *parfit gentil knyght.*
umbrage: shadow; but how much more resonant the antique form
new earth: Revelation XXI 1
Nature: The OVV 16-7 text has, as well as earlier *varia*, a less effective stanza 3
        which begins:

Nature, thy pardon I entreat / The simple tracking of her feet &c.

Beloved

Mortal, if thou art beloved,
Life's offences are removed:
All the fateful things that checkt thee,
Hearten, hallow, and protect thee.
Grow'st thou mellow? What is age?
Tinct on life's illumined page,
Where the purple letters glow
Deeper, painted long ago.
What is sorrow? Comfort's prime,
Love's choice Indian summer-clime.
Sickness? Thou wilt pray it worse
For so blessed, balmy nurse.
And for death? When thou art dying
'Twill be love beside thee lying.
Death is lonesome? Oh, how brave
Shows the foot-frequented grave!
Heaven itself is but the casket
For Love's treasure, ere he ask it,
Ere with burning heart he follow,
Piercing through corruption's hollow.
If thou art beloved, oh then
Fear no grief of mortal men!

T0244 The title appears only in a notebook index (OVC) for poems written in 1884,
but the relevant page (40) has been cut out. If this *is* the poem (which
seems reasonable), the context of dated poems suggests it may have been written
Aug/Oct 1884. It was already in print in *The Contemporary Review* by December
1885 (JCR 48 862, OYV 29). It is also not clear whose work it is; OVC seems almost
entirely Michael's *oeuvre*, but other autographs appear in Edith's hand in her own
special notebooks OVI and YFA. She certainly laid great store by it ('My beautiful
copy in a girl's handwriting' ZJW 217b), but neither assigned it to Michael, nor laid
claim to it herself if she was proud of it (as the dreadful T0405), which she often did
in the OVI text. Perhaps Michael is marginally the more likely author. The poem
deservedly appears in all three versions of UNDERNEATH THE BOUGH, from UTB 5.

Sickness? Edith read the piece to her dying mother, which seems awesomely
insensitive (*footnote* OVI 5b, ZJB 97a). Especially verse 13.

Shifting Faith

My God, Thou must not angry be
That though Thou art my happy shade,
In Thy dear dark I have no constant rest—
    Rest seems remote—
For see:
I sit here in the shadow of a boat
And as the sun doth lift
    My place I shift.
It is Thy movements that prevent
    My full content:
And as Thy stronger glory doth assail
    Old shelters fail
  Yet am I not dismayed;
    Yea, do with me,
My God as seemeth to Thee best;-
  Thy baffling heats I brave,
And here & there set up my temporal tent,
'Till; neath the night's securer firmament,
    I plant my grave

T0273   A single manuscript survives, an autograph in Michael's hand with the footnote *Aug & Sep 1885 (Hornsea & Runham?)*, one of thirty five poems in a black notebook of fair copies (OVD 45-6). Her letters to Edith indicate that in late August 1885 she had been in Great Yarmouth (OCA 113), and by 05 September she was writing from Runham Vicarage in the Norfolk Broads (OCA 115); she might have been visiting Alice Trusted (MFC 64), a life-long friend. All the pieces in OVD are of a religious temper, the notebook titled 'The Heavenly Love'. Here is Michael talking unaffectedly to a very real and personal God; even to the end of her life this simple faith, simple but by no means simplistic, stronger than rock, survived all the tempests that were to come. The title adumbrates a mischief and wit also inescapably part of the character of the 'Priest of the Family' (ZJN 69a).

(The death of Publia)

Hades is tongueless,
  Death hath no lyre;
Deep, deep the rest he gives
  From life's long tire,
Laying the fevered heart
  Far from desire.

He with oblivion
  Comes as a charm,
Nought that hath chanced to us
  Further can harm;
Passion, vicissitude,
  Break not our calm.

Fear of the future
  Ageing to-day,
Terrors of clinging love,
  Presage, dismay,
Senseless, distorting hope,
  Death puts away.

He is the Helper;
  What can transcend
His care that provideth
  For grief, an end,
For rest, eternity?
  Death is our friend.

T0281   Michael Field was at work on BRUTUS ULTOR in the autumn of 1885, and
the play was in print by April 1886. The plot chosen was a strong one: 'this
story of the father of the Roman republic' (XBU pe, 17 Feb 1886); it also
encompassed the familiar tragedy of Lucretia and the lustful Sextus Tarquinius.
Perhaps less well known was Brutus's delivery of his own sons up for execution, when
they joined a plot to restore the hated Tarquins. In the play, his rejected wife Publia
('I shall look on her no more') dies of a broken heart, clinging to the urn containing

Acheron

Elaia, my soul's bride,
Thou must not leave me!
Though 'tis a mournful land
Through which I travel,
I will but take thee by the hand,
    And be thy guide
To mysteries thou must in art unravel.
When thou a little way art gone,
Ere the grove's steep descent
Darkening can grieve thee,
Thou backward to the sweet stars shalt be sent;
    While I plod on
    To Acheron.

the ashes of her dead sons. Although a collaboration, Edith seems to have written the major part, so this death song for Publia (XBU V.iv) may well be hers.

no lyre: A reference to Hermes, who gave up his invention to Apollo; Hermes, as *Psychopompos*, is the Helper— the herald of Hades who summons the dying by a touch on the eyes with his golden rod.

T0286 This piece was written by Michael 04 October 1885, as the surviving autograph in her hand confirms (OVV 38b sa footnote). It was published in UNDERNEATH THE BOUGH, UTB 74-5; the first verse was discarded in the later BOUGH editions, and there were other varia.

Elaia: If this word is an interjection, it is outlandish even by Michael Field standards; if a proper name, its significance is uncertain. No classical precedent has been identified: (the nearest is Anius's maenad daughter *Elaïs*, her name meaning *olive oil*, which might briefly confuse only Popeye). It may be for this reason the *incipit* was dropped. In any case there seems little doubt the dedicatee was Edith.

thy guide: 'It is rather as a poet-rearer than a poet that I ask for fame' (Michael in a letter to Browning, ZCL 57r, 1886).

Acheron: The Stream of Woe, one of the tributaries of the River Styx in the Underworld; Michael, with her 39th birthday in sight, was becoming conscious of aging (sa T0275).

21

The all-wise bird sat questioning the moon:
'How is it thou dost give us but the boon
Of half thy radiant orb? There is one side
Unto my full reflecting eye denied.'

The moon a little fidgeted and drew
A passing cloud to hide her from the view:
'Oh, be content with what thou dost behold,
The gentle features and the smile of gold;
For on the other side— tears wouldst thou weep,
Minerva, couldst thou see the dreary steep:
'Tis a great warehouse of the things men lost,
Hairpins and scissors mixed with love starcrost,
The North-West Passage and the Wandering Jew,
Stuffed in with *whether Hamlet's mother knew
Of Hamlet's father's murder*— all that vexed,
And poor mortality in vain perplexed,
Is heaped up there, and none to dust the place
That warehouses the rubbish of your race.'

On the confessing moon the owl awhile
Gazed sadly, then her features broke in smile,
And, with a cynical slight flap of wing,
She said: 'Then learning is a dangerous thing,
And Solomon and I are right in this—
The Knowing know that Ignorance is Bliss.
I tell you there are bards— but let them gull
Their fellow mortals, lest life be too dull!'

So with a truism from Mr. Tupper
Minerva fell to mousing for her supper.

T0288   This jolly farrago first appeared in print when Elizabeth Sturge published *Reminiscences of My Life* in 1928; her brief introduction is worth recalling. Of Michael Field she wrote "Both were delightful women. Edith had the more ethereal grace, but Katherine was also very attractive and piquant, both in person and conversation. As an illustration of this side of her character I will quote a short *jeu d'esprit* which was sent to one of my cousins:

>   A Christmas card addressed to Sarah Jane Tanner,
>   after a discussion as to 'why we only see one side of the moon'.

N.B. 'The all wise bird' was a nickname ... for Katherine Bradley." (FES 38-9).

Elizabeth's fair copy seems to be based on that included in her cousin's rough notes for a talk to the Portfolio Society in Bristol some years previously (OZR 34). Sarah remembered of Michael Field in their 'Bristol days' "how they entered into the frivolity of our Christmas parties, which they nicknamed 'frisks'" (YCC 6-7). An Oxford manuscript also quotes the first eight verses (OZQ 63). Although clearly by Michael, accurate dating is much more difficult. December 1879 would have been their first Christmas in Stoke Bishop; by December 1884 they were at Stoke Green, and although the Bristol connection was strong to the end of the '80's (and see ZKE 32-3), it would seem 1885 is probably the latest date for the old nickname still to be current in face of the new 'Michael'.

all-wise bird:	Southey speaks of 'The Simorg.. the all-knowing Bird' (VTS XI 273-5), and Beckford also mentions 'The Simurgh.. that wonderful bird of the East' (VVB 51,145 fn). In various exotic spellings, mercifully eventually reduced to 'Sim', this *sobriquet* for Katharine appears in many family letters and the early volumes of the Journal (sa OZG 201r,T0153).
Minerva:	Roman goddess of wisdom, the equivalent of Athene, who sprang 'fully-armed' from the brain of Zeus. The owl was her special companion, presumably for its round-eyed gravity; an old name for Athene was *Glaucopis*, usually translated as 'grey-eyed', yet the root could equally be 'owl-eyed'; this has been thought to indicate earlier worship of the owl, perhaps in its more sinister nocturnal and underworld aspects.
NW Passage:	The Portuguese Corte Real attempted to find a sea-route round Canada to the Pacific in 1500, and in Elizabeth's reign the English hoped to find this shorter route to the East; but it was not till 1847 that Sir John Franklin actually discovered it, dying in the attempt. His splendidly named ships HMS *Erebus* and *Terror* were last seen in Lancaster Sound. Roald Amundsen made the first actual transit, east to west, in the sloop *Gjöa* in 1903-6. He achieved more lasting fame in December 1911 when he reached the South Pole.
Hamlet:	In all this, one must not forget the *Macbeth Murder Mystery*, which Selene has (naturally) overlooked. This was eventually solved only in the late 1930's by James Thurber.
Ignorance:	Closing verses of Thomas Gray's *Ode on a Distant Prospect of Eton College*: —where ignorance is bliss, /'Tis folly to be wise.
Mr. Tupper:	Presumably Martin Farquhar Tupper, 1810-89: his *Proverbial Philosophy: A Book of Thoughts and Arguments, Originally Treated* ran to four series (1838,42,67,69) and presented homespun reflections in a mixture of maxim and doggerel.

Primrose leaves

Not always with the Spring its joyance closes;
It is Midsummer, love, and while I pass
    Among forgotten things—
Dry oak-sprays, faded mosses, woodbine strings—
    The large, clear leaves of primroses
      Spread through the grass.

Not always with love's flower love perishes;
Long time our passion hath been dead, and still
    About my heart doth thrive
A memory of thee so green, so live
    A solemn power it cherishes
      To bless and thrill.

T0294   This poem was published in *The Spectator* in August 1888 (JSP #3137),
and was possibly written in June 1886 during a stay at Aville farm near
Dunster (M ZJM 147a, OCV 155). An autograph also exists in Edith's hand
(OVI 108), but the tone is unmistakeably Michael's. It is probably (but who can say
certainly?) a recollection of Alfred Gérente, whom she had lined up for matrimony in
late 1868; his sudden death closed that book for ever. But even as late as 1894 his
memory was still vivid: 'Goodness what a sentimental girl I was' (M ZJG 133b, sa
QFM 21). Edwin Essex loved this poem as an 'illustration' of Aquinas's principle of
causality, '...almost a paraphrase of his own words. How they came to stumble on
this principle unawares is one of the riddles of their superfine art' (JCM 239).

woodbine strings: The name "woodbine" has been applied to a variety of hedgerow
climbers such as Traveller's joy *Clematis vitalba* and bindweeds
of the Convolvulus family, as *Calystegia sepium*. But the plant
implied here is almost certainly Shakespeare's sweet honeysuckle
Lonicera periclymenum, the 'strings' being the climbing stems.
In winter these dry stems were at one time cut for smoking,
hence the alternative rural name "Boy's bacca".

Love's Orison

My lady hath a lovely rite:
When I am gone
No prayer she saith
As one in fear:
For orison,
Pressing her pillow white
With kisses, just the sacred number,
She turns to slumber;
Adding sometimes thereto a tear
And a quick breath.

T0295   Written by Michael at Clyde Banks in August 1886; a page from a tiny
          notebook in her hand still survives, probably the original autograph (OYR
          114). A footnote *To Pussie* confirms it was written for her niece, as does
Edith's own fair copy *Written by my Love* (OVI 14b sa ZJQ 72a). The poem was
published in UNDERNEATH THE BOUGH, UTB 76 as #14 in *The Third Book of
Songs*, the section specially concerned with Michael's poems to Edith.

hath: This became *has* in the revised edition of UNDERNEATH THE
                    BOUGH, UTC.
lovely rite: Edwin Essex was to comment in 1931 'Their lives .. they had
                    always observed as a "lovely rite"'. (JCM #8 243).
orison: prayer
sacred number: Almost certainly 3, the 'god number' in a variety of religions, from
                    the *Moerae* and Zeus/Poseidon/Hades of the Greeks to the
                    Trimurti of India and the Osiris/Isis/Horus Holy Family of Egypt.
                    Eventually, as with most other fables, the idea was assimilated in
                    the Trinity of christian myth. Three is a ritual number which is
                    observed in fairy and folk tales (as Goldilocks, the *Graeae*, Lear's
                    three daughters); it was still being applied in a context of 'kisses
                    three' as late as Edwardian society (perhaps even now).
                    Numerology is a fascinating minefield: other possibilities are 7
                    (witchcraft), 8 (Pythagoras) and 9 (the especially potent 3 x 3). But
                    these (and even higher) numbers are probably impractical for
                    regular bolster bussing. This is a beautiful poem.

(Long Ago VII)

Μὴ κίνη χέραδας·

Stir not the shingle with thy boat,
   It groans beneath the keel;
Still on the senseless waters float,
   Until thy heart can feel;

Keep to Ægæan tracts of fair,
   Invulnerable sea;
The land cries out in pain to bear
   One who from love is free.

Yea, linger 'mid the barren foam,
   Ungreeted, out of reach
Of those who watch the sailor home
   On Mitylene's beach.

Oh, I forget that Love's own Queen
   Is called the Ocean-born;
Forth from the wine-dark waves, first seen,
   She sprang in grace forlorn:

Forget that once across the sea,
   Thou, with thy swinging oar,
Did'st row the goddess mightily,
   Careless of coin, to shore.

She gave thee beauty— love's delight
   Would give thee. Sail away!
Learn from the natal waves her might,
   Then joyous seek the bay.

T0309   The Sappho fragment is #114 in Wharton's memoir: *Stir not the shingle*
(VSW 131). Michael wrote to Browning in April 1887 that Edith 'after more
than a year's silence suddenly became lyrical' (ZCL 89), yet 'about thirty' of
the Sapphic lyrics had been completed by October 1886 (ZCL 73r), among them
probably T0309 (ZCL 91). The poem appears early on in both surviving autographs

(OVF 6,OVG 8), OVF being the text that Browning received, and upon which he pencilled comments; so it could have been written by Michael in 1886. Yet she says in the April 1887 letter that Edith had been 'indexing & arranging' the texts, so both date and authorship are contestable. It was published in LONG AGO, LAG 10-1.

The story is the famous one related by Palaephătus, concerning the elderly boatman Phaon who ferried free an old crone to Mytilene, only to discover his kindness had been to 'the goddess' (Aphrodite) herself; she rewarded him with youth and beauty. The sting in the tail is that, having encountered the goddess, he presumably found mortal women less appealing. Sappho, who had fancied herself in with a chance, and passionately loved him, now found herself in the stale fish basket. After writing him numerous love poems to no avail, she is said to have thrown herself off a cliff into the sea, where she drowned.

thy boat: Sappho addresses Phaon
Ocean-born: Aphrodite, goddess of Love, arose from sea-foam off the island of Cythera. Sturge Moore omits these final three stanzas— which amounts to half the poem; and thereby jettisons the whole mythic underpinning (SMF 24).

It was at about this time that Michael received practical evidence that Aphrodite might still have plans for her as well. At the age of 39, on 14 February 1886, she received a valentine from a young man of 24. He was Francis Brooks, the eldest son of her cousin Frances Holinsworth Brooks. Frances's mother Mary had been the sister of Michael's father Charles; the brother and sister had married at a double ceremony in a nonconformist chapel (at Laurence Street, Birmingham) on 4th May 1834. When Emma and Frances in turn married James Cooper and John Brooks the two families remained close; Frances ("Cousin Fanny") had ten other children after Francis was born in July 1861. From the first he seems to have been fascinated by 'the all-wise bird' (T0288) and as the young people grew up, addressed Katharine and Edith as 'the Sacred Ones' (T1195), a reflection of their shared classical interests. In 1880 Francis went up to Balliol to read Classics; it is perhaps not too fanciful to think he was the second person Michael had guided to 'mysteries...in art' (T0286). When the valentine arrived she wrote to Fanny "There is much foolish romance in my knight that must for his sake be checked" (OCV 146o). She admitted she would 'like a lifelong friendship' (and this indeed she was to have). Charles Bradley had died before she was 16 months old, and Michael seems only to have been able to relate to 'father-figures' (such as Gérente, Ruskin, James Cooper), so poor Francis had little chance. (The one glaring exception was to be Ricketts, though in this case it was almost certainly his sparkling conversation and lively personality that she found pre-eminently irresistible; sa ZCL 244r). In 1887 Francis joined the Latin and Greek Department at University College, Bristol and settled in Clifton; but he still smouldered (sa OKC 84r). Edith talks of a 'stormy romance', and in 1895 he 'glances fierily at Mick when no-one is looking' (ZJH 156b). Even as late as August 1902 she described him as 'in the top of the old flame' (ZJQ 132b); that October he would be appointed to the Chair in Classics. Michael took this long-term attachment almost for granted ("The Balliol is entirely mine" OCA 124a); in matters of mind they were ideally suited. There seems little doubt, despite the substantial age-gap, that he was devoted to her— perhaps this was the problem; perhaps she hankered for a benevolent domination. One feels saddened that she may have missed the one window of opportunity that could have afforded them both a lasting happiness. But if they *had* outraged lace-curtain convention and married, what then of Michael Field?

(Long Ago VI)

Πάρθενον ἀδύφωνον

Erinna, thou art ever fair,
Not as the young springflowers,
We who have laurel in our hair—
Eternal youth is ours.
The roses that Pieria's dew
Hath washed can ne'er decline;
On Orpheus' tomb at first they grew,
And there the Sacred Nine;
'Mid quivering moonlight, seek the groves
Guarding the minstrel's tomb;
Each for the poet that she loves
Plucks an immortal bloom.
Soon as my girl's sweet voice she caught,
Thither Euterpe sped,
And, singing too, a garland wrought
To crown Erinna's head.

T0311   A poem with the same ambiguities of date and author as T0309; there are
two autographs, OVF 8 and OVG 7 (ZCL 91o). The Sapphic fragment is
#61 in Wharton's memoir: *A sweet-voiced maiden* (VSW 98) and the poem
was published in LONG AGO, LAG 9.

Erinna:	A famed lyric poetess and friend of Sappho, probably also referred to in Sapphic fragment #77, VSW 107 ('Eranna'). See also T0350.
laurel:	Sacred to Apollo, and because evergreen, symbolising immortality.
Pieria:	Legendary birthplace of the Muses, near Mount Olympus in Thessaly. The roses that grew there were said not to wither, and conferred lasting fame on their wearers. (Sapphic fragment #68, VSW 102).
Orpheus:	Torn apart by the Maenads, his head floated, still singing, down the river Hebrus to the sea; it fetched up on the shores of Lesbos. The Muses gathered up his limbs and buried them at Leibethra, near the foot of Mount Olympus; Calliope (v.i.) was his mother.
Sacred Nine:	The Muses, daughters of Zeus and Mnemosyne (or Air and Earth), the patrons and supreme exponents of poetry and music: *Calliope* epic poetry; *Clio* history; *Erato* love poetry; *Euterpe* music & lyric poetry; *Melpomene* tragedy; *Polyhymnia* sacred music; *Terpsichore* dance; *Thalia* comedy; *Urania* astronomy.

(Long Ago XI)

Ἄβρα δηὖτε παχῇᾳ σπόλᾳ ἀλλόμαν

Dreamless from happy sleep I woke,
On me the piercing sunlight broke,
I drank the laughter of the breeze
Divine, O Cypris, from thy seas,
Then lithely in thick robe I sprang;
To me it seemed my body sang—

"Death is an evil." Phaon bent
Above his nets, magnificent.
"The wise immortals never die."
Phaon grew conscious I stood by;
And, oh! to bury in thy wave,
Lethe, one day, the glance he gave!

T0315   The epigraph is Sapphic fragment #55 in Wharton's memoir: *Then
delicately in thick robe I sprang* (VSW 95)— though the fragment has
also been attributed to Alcaeus. There are problems with date and
primary author as   for T0309 (q.v.); all one can say with certainty, is that it was
written by April 1887. There are two autographs, (OVF 12,OVG 12) both in Edith's
hand; the theme continues that of T0309. It was published in LONG AGO, LAG 17.

Cypris: Another name for Aphrodite (the Cyprian), because of the transfer of her
cult from Cythera to Paphos in Cyprus.
lithely: Suggested by Browning, rather than their original *blithely (ZCL 91)*.
an evil: A second Sappho fragment (Wharton memoir #137) is used here:

ἢ ὥσπερ Σαπφώ, ὅτι τὸ ἀποθνῄσκειν κακόν   οἱ θεοὶ γὰρ οὕτω
κεκρίκασιν   ἀπέθνῃσκον γὰρ ἄν

*Death is evil; the Gods have so judged: had it been good, they would
die* (Quoted in Aristotle's *Rhetoric*, ii.23; VSW 145). See also T0344.
Lethe: The Underworld river of Forgetting.

29

(Long Ago XVII)

Πλήρης μὲν ἐφαίνετ' ἀ σελάννα,
αἰ δ' ὡς περὶ βῶμον ἐστάθησαν

Α Παρθενία, παρθενία, ποῖ με λίποισ' ἀποίχη;
Β Οὐκέτι ἥξω πρὸς σέ, οὐκέτι ἥξω'

The moon rose full: the women stood
As though within a sacred wood
Around an altar— thus with awe
The perfect, virgin orb they saw
Supreme above them; and its light
Fell on their limbs and garments white.
Then with pale, lifted brows they stirred
Their fearful steps at Sappho's word,
And in a circle moved around,
Responsive to her music's sound,
That through the silent air stole on,
Until their breathless dread was gone,
And they could dance with lightsome feet,
And lift the song with visions sweet.
Then once again the silence came:
Their lips were blanched as if with shame
That they in maidenhood were bold
Its sacred worship to unfold;
And Sappho touched the lyre alone,
Until she made the bright strings moan.
She called to Artemis aloud—
Alas, the moon was wrapt in cloud!—
"Oh, whither art thou gone from me?
Come back again, virginity!
For maidenhood still do I long,
The freedom and the joyance strong
Of that most blessèd, secret state
That makes the tenderest maiden great.
O moon, be fair to me as these,
And my regretful passion ease;
Restore to me my only good,
My maidenhood, my maidenhood!"
She sang: and through the clouded night

An answer came of cruel might—
"To thee I never come again."
O Sappho, bitter was thy pain!
Then did thy heavy steps retire,
And leave, moon-bathed, the virgin quire.

T0321 There are two autographs, as usual both in Edith's hand (OVF 20,OVG
21), but with the same ambiguities of date and author as T0309. As with
that poem, it must have been completed by April 1887 (ZCL 91o), an
inconvenient fact that cannot be bent to fit a 'metaphorical field' fantasy (JVP 33
142-3). It was published in LONG AGO, LAG 26-7. The epigraph consists of two
separate Sapphic fragments from the Wharton memoir. The first is #53 (VSW 94):
  The moon rose full, and the women stood as though around an altar.
The second is #109 (VSW 129):
  A *Maidenhood, maidenhood, whither art thou gone away from me?*
  B *Never again will I come to thee, never again.*
There are allusions to three other fragments in the text.

virgin orb: The moon is sacred to Artemis.
pale: Sapphic fragment #100 reads
    And a soft (paleness) is spread over the lovely face
circle: Sapphic fragment #54 (VSW 95) begins
    Thus at times with tender feet the Cretan women dance in
    measure round the fair altar,
dance: Sapphic fragment #54
blanched: See Sapphic fragment #100 above, also *moon-bathed* in v38.
Artemis: Apollo's twin sister, goddess of the chase, but eternally chaste: the maiden
  huntress whose silver bow is the new moon. Her companion nymphs
  are also expected to pursue anything on four legs, but avoid dalliance
  with all eager applicants on two. Confusingly, she is also the goddess of
  childbirth, a sort of patron saint of midwives. Which smacks of one
  familiar definition of a teacher. She is known to the Romans as Diana,
  and as such appears in the beautiful T0994; the whole troupe are
  celebrated in the Michael Field masque NOONTIDE BRANCHES (sa
  T0763).
do I long: An inversion of Sapphic fragment #102
    Do I still long for maidenhood?
cruel: For the cruelty of Artemis, one need look no further than the legend of
  Actæon.
quire: choir

(Long Ago XVIII)

Τὸν δ' ἐπιπλάζοντες ἄμοι φέροιεν καὶ μελεδώναις

Boreas, leave thy Thracian cave,
Cross the grey, up-tossing wave;
With thy lips, rough-bearded, swell
All the voices of thy shell.
Chase the wheat-producing mist,
That the teeming furrows kissed;
With thy morning breath drive forth
Every dense cloud of the north;
Let thy chilly blasts prevail,
Make the shivering olive pale,
Hold the sailor in the bay,
Sweep distress and care away!
Let thy winds, wide-wandering, bleak,
Dry the tears on Sappho's cheek!
Buffeting with gusts, constrain
Woes of love to quit my brain:
Bind them on thy pinions strong,
Bear them on thy course along.
Come, stern god, and set me free;
Rival Eros' tyranny!
Then, exultant, I will praise,
Now at banquets, now in lays,
Thee, fierce Thracian, gentle grown,
And thy mighty godhead own.

T0322   This was written by Edith probably sometime in the early Spring of 1887
(M ZCL 94r). The Sappho fragment is #17 in Wharton's memoir:
According to my weeping: it and all care let buffeting winds bear away
(VSW 72). Edith developed it outwards from the core verses 12-5. Two autographs
survive (OVF 22,OVG 23); the poem was published in LONG AGO, LAG 28-9.

Boreas: The North Wind is one of the four sons of Astraeus and Eos.
Thracian cave: In Mount Haemus, to which he abducted Oreithyia, an Athenian
                princess; he later helped the Athenians by destroying Xerxes's ships.
Rival Eros: Boreas is well known as a fertiliser, especially of mares.

(Queen Mary's Song)

Ah, I, if I grew sweet to man
It was but as a rose that can
No longer keep the breath that heaves
And swells among its fluttering leaves.

The pressing fragrance would unclose
The flower, and I became a rose,
That, unimpeachable and fair,
Planted an odour in the air.

No art I used men's love to draw;
I lived but by my being's law,
As roses are by heaven designed
To bring the honey to the wind.

I found there is scant sun in spring;
I found the blast a riving thing;
And yet even ruined roses can
No other than be sweet to man.

T0347   Mary Stuart, one of history's more tiresome figures, though she made a
good end. Or beginning. The song occurs in Act III.i of THE TRAGIC MARY;
the Queen is walking through the garden at Craigmillar (XTM 94-5). The
piece was regularly reworked for subsequent appearances in UNDERNEATH THE
BOUGH (UTB 25,UTC-D). It is first seen in a draft in Michael's hand for the whole
scene, dated 15 September 1887 (OQH 24). There are three other autographs,
including one in Edith's special book (OVI 51); this has a footnote, confirmed by a
Journal entry, that she read the poem to her mother on 14 August 1889 (ZJB 97a).
But the OQH autograph seems strong evidence that Michael was the actual author.

Ah, I: In UNDERNEATH THE BOUGH, this became the less unusual *Ah me;* in
verse 4, *fluttering* was replaced by *folded;* and verse 15 lost the
introductory *And.*

an odour: The 'revised and decreased' edition of UNDERNEATH THE BOUGH (UTC)
additionally reads: *Planted its sweetness in the air* ; and loses the entire
stanza 4. This is also the version that Sturge Moore published (SMF 26).

33

(Long Ago XLIV)

Οὔ τι μοι ὔμμες

Nought to me! So I choose to say:
We meet, old friends, about the bay;
The golden pulse grows on the shore—
Are not all things as heretofore
Now we have cast our love away?

Men throng us; thou art nought to me,
Therefore, indifferent, I can see
Within thine eyes the bright'ning grace
That once thou gavest face to face;
'Tis natural they welcome thee!

Nought to me, like the silver ring,
Thy mislaid, worthless gift. Last spring,
As any careless girl, I lost
The pin, yet, by the tears it cost,
It should have been worth cherishing.

Nought, nought! and yet if thou dost pass
I grow as summer-coloured grass,
And if I wrap my chiton round,
I know thine eye hath caught the sound,
Although thou heedest not, alas!

Nought to me! Wherefore dost thou throw
On me that glittering glance, as though,
Friend, I had ever done thee wrong,
When the crowd asks me for the song,
"Atthis, I loved thee long ago"?

T0357   This poem does not appear within the set sent to Browning by April
1887; indeed, it is in the '2nd Series' (OVF 51), perhaps among those
'9 or 10 new ones which I shall ask leave to send you in the Spring' (a
letter from Michael dated 31 December 1887, ZCL 120o). But it was apparently only
at 05 May 1888 that she posted him '18 more fragments, of which 8 are the work
of Erinna *(ICT: Edith)*' (ZCL 147-8). The present piece seems most likely to have been

written within these extreme dates. Again, one cannot be certain who is the author, but one's instinct is that it was more likely to be Michael. Autographs exist at OVF 72 (annotated by Browning), and OVG 60. The poem was published in LONG AGO, LAG 70-1; the epigraph is Sapphic fragment #23 in Wharton's memoir: *Ye are nought to me* (VSW 75). This fragment was also used within Long Ago XXXIV (T0337).

golden pulse: Here a second Sapphic fragment is being used, #30 in the memoir:

χρύσεοι δ' ἐρέβινθοί ἐπ' ἀϊόνων ἐφύοντο

And golden pulse grew on the shores. Wharton elaborates 'Quoted by Athenaeus, when he is speaking of vetches' (VSW 81). This fragment is the major basis for Long Ago IV (T0390); also in T0308.

face to face: And here a third (Wharton memoir #29):

Στᾶθι κἄντα φίλος . . . .
καὶ τὰν ἐπ' ὄσσοις ἀμπέτασον χάριν

Stand face to face, friend . . . and unveil the grace in thine eyes. Athenaeus 'says Sappho addressed this to a man who was admired above all others for his beauty' This man has been variously hypothesised as Phaon, the groom in a bridal song, or even her brother (VSW 80).

chiton: The Greek tunic, a shirt-like body garment.
Atthis: This is a fourth Sapphic fragment (Wharton memoir #33):

Ἠράμαν μὲν ἔγω σέθεν, Ἄτθι, πάλαι πότα

I loved thee once, Atthis, long ago (VSW 83). Wharton quotes Suidas, that Atthis was one of Sappho's three companions and friends (VSW 22), and observes that the poet was jealous when Atthis 'flitted' to Andromeda (Sapphic fragment #41). Atthis is specifically addressed in Long Ago XIV (T0318) and occurs in three other of the lyrics. Edith briefly became identified with Atthis (ZCL 94,9; ZKD 90a).
long ago"?: There is little doubt LONG AGO was named for this line. In the published text, the question mark is included within the quotation comma, which makes no literal or syntactic sense; I therefore agree with Sturge Moore (SMF 65)— for once!— in correcting what is evidently a typographical error.

Robert Browning, residing at this time at 29 De Vere Gardens, Palace Gate, is said to have wanted Michael Field 'to come & live near him' (ZJO 129b). This may account for a removal from Bristol to Reigate in Surrey in April 1888. Their new home was Blackboro' Lodge "we boldly hope to transform the name into Blackberry" (the blackberry, in fruit and flower, symbolised the 'united life'— aunt and niece—of Michael Field as far back as 1881 sa MFC 65). Michael described the house in a letter to Browning: "a secluded garden, & a study from which there are pleasant glimpses of... hills... there is a windmill hard by... we have, I think, a fair prospect of happiness " (ZCL 130or). On 14 April 1888 Michael made the first entry in the first volume of the monumental Journal which was to become WORKS AND DAYS.

The Shut of Flowers

Bury her at even,
That the stars may shine
  Soon above her,
And the dews of twilight cover:
  Bury her at even,
  Ye that love her.

Bury her at even,
At the shut of flowers
  Softly take her;
They will lie beside nor wake her:
  Bury her at even
  At the shut of flowers.

Bury her at even
In the wind's decline;
  Night receive her
Where no noise may ever grieve her!
  Bury her at even,
  And then leave her!

T0397 Written 11 June 1889, almost certainly by Edith (ZJB 77a); this seems to
have been the only occasion the title was used. The poem, an early
success, was published almost immediately in *The Academy* (JAC #894,
22 June;OYV 44), and eventually in UNDERNEATH THE BOUGH, UTB 41-2. In
1928 it was even set to music (VPH). The poem was 'Written of little Evelyn Barrett'
(OVI 12), a child niece of their Clifton friend Isabelle Wedmore; she had died some
four days earlier (ZJB 76b). Michael wrote in a letter 'Her wise parents did not speak
to her of death. But she found the way to it— a babe in the wood— all by herself'
(ZCC 215-6). Edith had been writing *Songs of Sundry Natures* (OVI), a 'new &
beautiful Elizabethan song-book which aspires to treat of Victorian themes in
Elizabethan temper' (M ZCC 225r), and a few months later reapplied the poem to
the death of her own mother (OVI 12 *footnote; Worlds Away*, YFA 7-8). Sturge
Moore, writing of the poem in the preface of his anthology of Michael Field poems,
remarked 'met at unawares, (it) might set one hunting the Elizabethans for the
satisfying author's name, to conclude that there must be an important one unknown'
(SMF 15); this however did not deter him from dropping stanza two. Evelyn also
appeared in T0396 (sa OCY 88-98; and second note to T0947) .

A rose
That throws
All her sweet my way,
Though she grows
In the toils of a trellis, in durance & drouth,
   On the other side the pale.
O gallant, the frail
Rare creature to scale
High walls, till she flingeth free
Her beauty, her blossoms down to me,
To me the pride of the damask mouth.
   Does she love the South?—
Can I say her nay?
Thy triumph, thy splendour hail!

T0399 An untitled poem known only from a single draft in the Journal (ZJB 79b); it
        is dated 19 June 1889, and is in Michael's hand. Michael (for it is surely
        her work) then almost immediately reworked the original idea into a more
conventional 'art' poem similar to some of the lyrics of Herrick; the rose becomes a
'lady', the trellis 'bonds that tie her', the writer 'honest Corin' (T0400). This was
eventually printed in UNDERNEATH THE BOUGH, UTB 23. The original sketch, here
in print for the first time, may be less crafted; but it is certainly much more vivid and
arresting. Michael was to write at least one other memorable poem about a rose,
The Grand Mogul (T0637).

drouth: drought
pale: fence
Can I... ? A verse which underwent three drafts, from an original:
                Oh the wild, warm sway! —

'Twas in his wanderings far from native Thrace
I saw him— in a secret, leafy place:
Spring was just flashing out; black poplars stood
In golden leafage 'gainst the ilex-wood,
From wh: he issued, on his brows a scowl
Of anger at Athene's haunting owl,
And sat him down & brooded, till an oak
Pushed its young saplings toward him, & he broke
The sunny twigs & smiled: I knew him then—
Nature's fond, liberating God, & when
Solemn from grassy-pillowed, gurgling throat
He boomed out on the air his Evian note,
Prompter than echo's voice my blood replied,
I sprang convulsive up the mountain-side

Easeful he shouted— from the forest height
A sudden, lovely, clamorous concourse bright
Leapt to his side— no vision, no vain dream.
I felt within the vital madness teem,
To join that fearless band; not even could Love
Though as a strong wind rushing from above,
So clear a passage for the spirit free,
As then my quickened senses made for me:
Eyesight & hearing with a finer lust
And apprehension were endowed, & just
As Dryope at threshold of her beech
Stood with lips growing human— out of reach
The great train through a rocky fissure wound;
I woke alone on the sun-broidered ground.

T0415   This draft only exists as a single Journal autograph in Edith's hand, and is
almost certainly her work; undated, it was probably written in late summer
1889 (ZJB 127b). The draft has no title, and shows less punctiliousness with
the mythological niceties than is usual with Michael Field. Such matters would
probably have been resolved on later editing; what is really interesting is that this
may be a first inkling of the projected IO BACCHE! of 1895 (ZJJ 56a).

After an initial ambiguity, the 'liberating God' emerges as Dionysus, though he is not commonly associated with the oak (v7-9) and beech (v25), trees of the sacred grove of Dodona, the oracle of Zeus. The loud voice (v11-2) and shout (v15) are also more a characteristic of Pan. Later poems show Edith was well aware of these points (T0935,64); the oak sapling may be intended to remind the wanderer of his father.

native Thrace:	Though a common assertion, the cult of Dionysus seems most likely to have originated in Phrygia, where *Diounsis* is named as son of an earth goddess *Zemelo*. This story seems an obvious antecedent of the Semele myth, which makes him the son of Zeus, and marks his actual birthplace as Thebes. His wandering was the result of madness induced by a Hera furious at yet another of Zeus's infidelities (v.i.)
owl:	See the note to T0288 (Minerva).
sunny:	The autograph word is scrawled and difficult to read; other less likely possibilities are *shiny* and *shining*. If the word is correct, it is just possibly an elliptic allusion to the fiery brilliance that incinerated his mother Semele. Which may be why the writer 'knew him then'.
Evian:	Presumably after the blood-chilling Maenadic cries of *Evoe!* (ɛvoɩ) emitted during their drunken maraudings. Not a mineral water. Far from it.
echo:	A nymph who again is more closely associated with Pan; for abetting Zeus in his dalliance with the mountain nymphs (all of them), by telling his consort Hera distracting interminable stories, Hera cursed her with the inability to say anything at all, that had not first been said by someone else. This greek *Shīrazād* eventually pined away after her scornful rejection by Narcissus, who understandably tired of having his every word repeated. Eventually only her voice was left. As to this day.
concourse:	Any lingering doubt as to the god in question is now finally resolved. The rites of Dionysus were celebrated by gangs of loutish women (the Maenads) who, after an initial restrained drinking, singing and processing, rampaged through the mountains dismembering and devouring any living thing in their path. As one author puts it "in the fervent illusion they were devouring the god and thus communing with him". This daft idea re-emerged in other 'religions' and incredibly still lingers. Other members of the troupe were woodland spirits, the Pan-like satyrs and sileni (wise, but lushes and lechers to a goat). By the time the cults reached Rome, the 'rites' eventually ameliorated into the Bacchanalian orgies open to all comers. A strange, almost comical, vision to capture the imagination of a young Victorian lady.
strong wind:	An allusion presumably to Acts II 2.
Dryope:	A hapless nymph seduced by Apollo in the guise of a tortoise; she was later changed to a black poplar (a possible echo of v3) or perhaps a lotus tree. The reference to a beech is mystifying, as is the implication that the metamorphosis is here going into reverse (v26); (wine was however apparently drunk from beechwood bowls in the rites). Edith had already written a poem on the Dryope/tortoise myth (T0371).
human:	As with *sunny* (v9), this word is difficult to read. Were it actually *humous*, (of the earth) this might indicate the metamorphosis was at least going in the right direction, but then the meaning is more rather than less obscure.

But even with the ambiguities, this is an amazing and exciting poem.

Meeting and Farewell

Ah me, how sadder than to say farewell
    It is to meet
Dreading that Love hath lost his spell
    And changed his sweet!
I would we were again to part,
    With that full heart.

The hawthorn was half-bud, half-flower,
    At our goodbye;
And braver to me since that hour
    Are earth and sky:
My God, it were too poor a thing
    To meet this spring.

Our hearts— life never would have marge
    To bear their tides,
Their confluent rush! Lo, death is large
    In boundary-sides;
And our great χαῖρε must be said
    When I am dead.

T0446   There are two autographs, the first in Michael's hand in the Journal, dated
07 May 1890 (ZJC 33b); the second a fair copy in Edith's special book
(OVI 69b). Edith specifically assigns the poem to 'Sim', which was an old
family name for Katharine (see the first note to T0288). In any case there is little
doubt this piece is by Michael: apart from the Greek tag, there are fingerprints in the
characteristic metre-filling interjections. Her sister (Edith's mother) had died the
previous August; but her own mother's wedding anniversary had just passed (04
May), and the 22nd anniversary of her death was approaching (30 May). One could
argue convincingly that Emma (Harris) Bradley is the ghost troubling her. Yet Robert
Browning, whom she *might* have seen a last time in May 1889, and whose tomb she
had just visited in Westminster Abbey, seems the most probable subject (he had died
in Venice in December). The poem was published with the above title in *The
Academy* that same May (JAC #943) and then reprinted (JLA #186); but all three
UNDERNEATH THE BOUGH editions omit the title (UTB 34; as #5 in *The Second
Book of Songs*, which treats of the deaths of both Browning and Emma Cooper).

hawthorn: The may would have been blooming in May 1889 (*and* in 1868), as it
               was at the time she wrote this poem.
χαῖρε: Welcome, greeting, salute; (cf 'two dear, *Greek* women' ZJB 4b).

Nella trista valle

Dark-headed Poet, Wanderer of the lute,
With thy young lover's voice so fresh in woe
For passion of three thousand years ago,
When do we find thee sweetest? In pursuit
Of thy Eurydice; or in thy mute
Rapture at finding her, when thou dost throw
Thy scarf about her, and compel her so
Unseen to fondle thee? Or in thy suit
To Pluto? Nay, I think, we love thee most
Bearing thy limpid music through the host
Of chaos, till the roar begins to wane;
For thou deliverest the fiends from pain
With thy soft motions, and henceforth for aye
We shall see Hades, Orpheus standing by.

T0475　　The first of four Italian sonnets (T0475-8) on the theme of Orpheus and
Eurydice, with the general title *Orfeo: to Signorina Giulia Ravogli*. They
are all in the hand of Michael, and almost certainly her work. The single
autograph is dated 04 December 1890 (ZJC 121b). *The Contemporary Review* was
not interested (ZJC 126b), but the Century Guild *Hobby Horse*, probably through the
influence of Selwyn Image, printed the set in January (JHH #21 35-8;OYV 55-7).

That summer had been eventful, with Edith's first venture abroad, publication of THE
TRAGIC MARY, and meetings with Wilde and George Moore. On 23 July James
bought Durdans; on 24 November Michael Field attended a lecture by Walter Pater.
It was on this occasion that Edith wrote in the Journal 'Selwyn Image came up & told
us there was a great opportunity we must not miss— Orfeo at the Italian Opera'
(ZJC 120a). The following Saturday 'we went...to hear Julia Ravogli as Orfeo'; Edith
then proceeds to a detailed review. Ravogli impressed: 'Her hands are as expressive
as a countenance'; but not all else pleased. '..the scene was unutterably vulgar; the
tomb of Euridice marked with her name like an advertisement, & ballet girls in puffed
tulle advancing with wreaths....The Euridice in the last Act was irritating, obvious— a
big woman without imagination or sensitiveness...' (ZJC 122b). But the following
April, Edith went to see the opera again (ZJD 30a), with 'my beloved Ravogli as
Orpheus' (OCY 117r). See also MFC front cover (OYS 19o) and MFC 59.

Nella trista valle:　　In the valley of sorrows, or (more loosely), vale of torments.
Poet:　　　　　　　　Orpheus; the story of his unsuccessful attempt to rescue his dead
wife Eurydice from Hades (Pluto) is perhaps sufficiently well known.

An Invitation

Come and sing, my room is south;
Come, with thy sun-governed mouth,
Thou wilt never suffer drouth,
    Long as dwelling
In my chamber of the south.

On the wall there is woodbine,
With its yellow-scarlet shine;
When my lady's hopes decline,
    Honey-smelling
Trumpets will her mood divine.

There are myrtles in a row;
Lady, when the flower's in blow,
Kisses passing to and fro,
    From our smelling,
Think, what lovely dreams will grow!

There's a lavender settee,
Cushioned for my sweet and me;
Ah, what secrets there will be
    For love-telling,
When her head leans on my knee!

Books I have of long ago
And to-day; I shall not know
Some, unless thou read them, so
    Their excelling
Music needs thy voice's flow:

Campion, with a noble ring
Of choice spirits; count this wing
Sacred! all the songs I sing
    Welling, welling
From Elizabethan spring:

French, that corner of primrose!
Flaubert, Verlaine, with all those
Precious, little things in prose,
    Bliss-compelling,
Howsoe'er the story goes:

All the Latins *thou* dost prize!
Cynthia's lover by thee lies;
Note Catullus, type and size
    Least repelling
To thy weariable eyes.

And for Greek! Too sluggishly
Thou dost toil; but Sappho, see!
And the dear Anthology
    For thy spelling.
Come, it shall be well with thee.

T0489   Written and completed by Michael 22 January 1891 (OVI 72-3,OVV 51-3);
    the original title was *The poet's invitation to his lady to visit him* (ZJD 7-8).
    Published UTB 80-2, Bottomley's 'poem I love most ' (ZCA 226r, MFC 56).
They would not move from Blackboro' Lodge to Durdans until 03 March (ZJD 24).

south: 'The South room is the Study at Durdans' (M OCZ 105r). It was
    eventually to be photographed in March 1899, just before the final
    (momentous) removal to Paragon (ZJN 47b,*OYS 22-3).
governed: 'The study is very small, but full of sun' (H OCY 116).
woodbine: 'Edith & Amy are already planning Morris's honeysuckle paper for the
    new study' (M ZCD 47r,71;ZJP 60b). See also the note to T0294.
myrtles: Ricketts commented 'You have real myrtles' on the first visit of 'The
    Painters' in May 1894 (ZJG 46a).
settee: 'a settle designed by Herbert Horne' (ZCD 82r sa MFC 59). 'Someday we
    will be taken in our settle, so Heaven, through our publishers, prosper
    us!-- taken, each with a lily in his right hand' (M ZCD 103r).
Books: The early draft has an alternative stanza 5 which refers to the Journal:
            There are books; and once we planned
            Such deep studies, come , command
            WORKS & DAYS: To understand
                Trouble-quelling
            Homer I must have your hand.
Verlaine: Michael Field attended his Barnard's Inn reading 22 November 1893;
    their special interest perhaps acquired from Symons (ZJF 93b,MFC 64).
Catullus: 'I am rereading Catullus & praising Michael constantly for the sound
    teaching in Latin she gave me' (H OCH 83r).
Anthology: The Greek Anthology.
spelling: Never a strong point with Edith! (OCK 33o,OZF 123).

43

Grave-mould

Yonder slope of sunny ground
One day by a fence was bound;
First it felt within its soil
Digging mortals sing and toil;
Then a weight was lowered deep,
And the grave became a heap
On an earth that only knew
What it was to feed on dew;
Zephyr touched its wayward flowers,
Birds had tripped on it for hours,
Life, she spun its grass intact,
Till Death wrought the delver's act.

Now no more the sunny slope
Lies in its own bloom and hope,
For an alien power destroys
Its unheedful, perfect joys.
Mortals dig at night and noon,
Grave near grave is huddled soon;
While across the jocund grass
Doom and lamentation pass:
Sorrow lingers round the place.
Innocent of drear disgrace,
It had lived beneath no blame
When but birds and zephyr came.

Youth— ah, youth, it is a field
We would never, never yield
To intrusion of the grave,
'Tis an acre we would save!
Yet one day a mound we see
Breaking its stability,
And the knowledge that is strange
Hath begun to spoil and change
Sweetness that was never bred
From remembrance of the dead,
But by nature had been sown,
As are greeny banks unmown.

One by one the tombs are pressed
In the boundaries of our breast;
Every year the native charm
Of our being suffers harm;
What it had not held before
It must cherish more and more,
Till we scarcely breathe a breath
That is ignorant of death;
For our flowers as we grow old,
Saddened, live on burial mould,
And the earth in us is made
Fruitful by the sexton's spade.

T0494 was completed by Edith 31 January 1891; she writes in the 'fair copies' heavy black book of early Michael Field poems that it 'came to me' (OVI 75b). The title is that of the Journal draft (ZJD 12ab); it was published untitled as the twelfth number of *The Second Book of Songs* in the original UNDERNEATH THE BOUGH (UTB 42-4), but not reprinted in the later editions.

Her mother (Michael's elder sister) had died 20 August 1889, and it is probable (since Emma Cooper's birthday, 01 February, was imminent) that the poem is a memory of her grave at Gatton near Reigate. But it is equally possible the piece is a literary exercise, a curious conceit on Edith's own 'alias', arising either opportunely in the writing, or as a deliberate departure point. In this respect a couplet from the discarded draft has a special wry charm:

> Thus we learn that we shall be
> Field no more but cemetery.

The idea persists fugitively in the opening of stanza three.

The death of Emma Cooper had left the way open for the removal in 1891, though the family did not go too far. Durdans, where they were to settle in a few weeks time, was in Wray Park Road. Michael wrote to John Miller Gray "Our new home Durdans is a nice little detached house in Reigate- with a garden all one can desire, & three sitting rooms" (ZCD 65r). This was to be their home for eight years. Edith certainly had no regrets (OCK 165o).

Saint Katharine of Alexandria

Bartolommeo Veneto

The Städel'sche Institut at Frankfurt

A little wreath of bay about her head,
The Virgin-Martyr stands, touching her wheel
With finger-tips that from the spikes of steel
Shrink, though a thousand years she has been dead.
She bleeds each day as on the day she bled;
Her pure, gold cheeks are blanched, a cloudy seal
Is on her eyes; the mouth will never feel
Pity again; the yellow hairs are spread
Downward as damp with sweat; they touch the rim
Of the green bodice that to blackness throws
The thicket of bay-branches sharp and trim
Above her shoulder: open landscape glows
Soft and apart behind her to the right,
Where a swift shallop crosses the moonlight.

T0507   By October 02 1891 they were visiting Frankfurt, and may have seen this
painting on Sat October 03. From the descriptive notes by Edith (now
'Heinrich', soon to be 'Henry') ZJD 118b, Michael seems to have written
the poem (dated October 10, ZJD 125b); the eponymous heroine was probably of
special interest to her. The sonnet was published in SIGHT AND SONG, SAS 31.

wreath of bay: Years after (15 January 1909), in a letter from Lansdowne House to
Michael, Ricketts wrote teasingly "Patience, the humblest but not the
most negligible of virtues, must now be added to your crown of
qualities (sometimes hidden by the wreath of bays)". VCR 26.

Virgin-Martyr: Katharine (or Catherine) of Alexandria (or Cyprus) at the age of 18
(allegedly) "managed to confound fifty philosophers in a religious
debate". This would explain the wreath of bay, a traditional award
for excellence. Understandably exasperated at this public nuisance
the emperor Maxentius had her put to the torture on a spiked wheel
now commemorated pyrotechnically. However she remained
stubbornly cheerful and argumentative, until in desperation he had
her beheaded. Angels (we are told) obligingly carried the body to
Mt. Sinai. There is not a shred of evidence that this little miss
know-it-all ever existed, which is probably just as well.

shallop: A boat, originally large and heavy, with one or more masts; later,
possibly as here, small and light in the sense of a dinghy.

On seeing a letter of Nelson's

Of all the passionate love-notes that have lain
In women's bosoms, & give dateless pain
Best of its kind— a doubt there cannot be—
This letter from a seaman on the sea:
Emma, beloved— I cannot even read
Your letter, so with favouring wind we speed:
God grant us soon to meet. May Heaven cheer
Your Horatia, — all who hold us dear—
Being ever, ever, ever— Then the name,
All hers, that is for ever England's fame.
And, for address a headland seen in faint
Outline. O eyes that Romney loved to paint
A Maenad's or a Love's, if he instead
Had caught your colour when that page was read.

T0542   A Journal autograph (and surely her work) in Michael's hand, dated 29
May 1892 (ZJE 93a). This quatorzain is an excellent example of Michael's
penchant for taking up prose and fitting it to poetry (sa T0551). On the
facing Journal page she copies the actual letter, an opportunity to see her skills in
action. She was to write of Nelson again (T1297), perhaps less successfully.

> My beloved Emma,
> I cannot even read your dear letter. We have fair wind and God will
> I hope soon grant us a happy meeting. The wind is quite fair & fresh
> We go too swift for the boat. May Heaven bless you & Horatia with
> all those who hold us dear to them
> for a short time farewell
>   Ever ever ever yours
>
>   Nelson   L. Brooks

Emma: Lady Hamilton

Horatia: Their daughter was born c 29 January 1801, an event which was of
superlative joy to him. She was still only four when he died at Trafalgar
21 October 1805; some of his last words were "Never forget Horatia".
Proud of her illustrious father, she lived to be over 80 (ob 06 March
1881), yet denied to the last that Lady Hamilton was her mother.

Romney: George Romney painted her often (she was a noted beauty) in romantic
guises as diverse as Circe and St. Cecilia. His picture of her as a
bacchante (that would have pleased Michael) may have been the locket
portrait that Nelson wore at his death on the *Victory*. Emma died in
1815.

On Dosso Dossi's Circe

How terrible this country, how
   Alone these creatures round a girl
     Herself now solitary:
For the mere quietness doth allow
     The heron in the swamp to curl
His neck & fish; nor be
     Vexed by that girl with changeless brow.

Her hand is on a runic stone
Pressed flat, & what is written there
     Is in her eyes, her breath,
Though to her very self unknown:
The homestead peeping unaware
     Admonishes of death—
So undisturbed, so overgrown.

Wild beasts that once were men have met
In circle by her— stag & doe,
     Daft howlet, & grey dog—
In the deep roadway lions forget
Their wrath:— a frolic puppy so
     Is cowed that as a log
He stretches where he first was set.

Her cloak has July's depth of green:
   Her hair that strays is scarce, & bound
     With flowerets pale & red
In double blinking wreath half seen
     Against the piny shade profound;
And her averted head
     Faces the gray-lit, open ground.

What fresh but ancient awe exhales
From her sweet silence, & is caught
     By fir-tree, deer & bird!
If men would catch it, naught avails
     Save to forget the strife of thought
Turn into brutes & dream unstirred
     For hours within the humming dales.

T0544   A Journal fair copy in Michael's hand 'written out' 19 June 1892. However the piece is affirmed as Henry's work, which Michael states she has "snatched up & rescued"; she confesses she has 'been brute to it— .... but here it is unhurt', so one may assume the poem is entirely as Henry left it (ZJE 102-3 rt H 92ab sa 42b-3a). There is an additional stanza, written opposite s2 but then struck out:

> Is this the Circe who with wine
> Enchants & dulls? She cons no book
> Child of Oceanid
> And Helios, she feels the brine
> Beyond the streams, & loves to look
> For what the sun has hid
> Within the substance of the pines

In February that same year Henry had made a list of fourteen paintings for a Second Series of SIGHT AND SONG 'by Heaven's grace' (ZJE 48a). Of these, only a draft for Mantegna's *Ecce Homo* (T0456), and the Dosso Dossi, appear to have survived. One can see why Michael "mouthed & mammocked" the *Circe* piece (something is amiss with the metrics of v7, and v17 is vintage Michael Field fustian), but in the light of some of the worst turgidities of SAS this has the makings of a fine poem.

Circe:	A witch-goddess, the daughter of Helios and Persa (and hence granddaughter of Oceanus), she had no love of men. Luckless sailors castaway on her Island of Aeaea ("Wailing") she drugged and transformed to beasts. In love with the seagod Glaucus (who preferred Scylla), in a jealous rage she is said to have turned the erstwhile beautiful girl into a monster with six dogs' heads. Pleasant lady. sa *Circe at Circaeum*, T1014.
peeping unaware:	This phrase replaces *underneath the pear*, which is scored out in the journal (ZJE 102b).
admonishes:	The 'homestead' seems unlikely to be Circe's palace.
sweet silence:	This also may appear out of character. Dosso Dossi and Ludovico Ariosto were close contemporaries, and the latter's *Orlando Furioso* features two other sorceresses, the wicked Alcina and the benevolent Melissa. Melissa overturns Alcina's spells, and it has been suggested that this painting actually depicts Melissa (Schlosser 1900). Matters are not made easier by the fact that Dosso Dossi attempted this subject at least twice, the better-known version being in the *Galleria Borghesa*.

The sudden obsession with turning paintings into poems seems to have originated in Paris in 1890 with an introduction to Bernhard Berenson, a social climber and self-styled authority on Italian pictures. By the following spring, they were attending his lectures at the National Gallery ("He belongs to the destructive school" ZCD 82o)– undeterred by the continual presence of his "hostess" Mrs. Mary Costelloe ("a comely young creature" ZJD 19b). That June the couple were even received at Durdans, and their new friends were most solicitous during the traumatic scarlet fever episode in Dresden later that summer. SIGHT AND SONG, the 'catalogue' of picture-poems, came out in May 1892, and June was to find Berenson and all three women once more in Paris, Michael Field paying him a retainer for Art lessons (a nice little earner).

He has told me all his love:-
All his love for my beautiful friend:
We pause: we are just at the end
Of a lane, by a weedy stile;
And he says, speaking swiftly, while
The thistledown sails through the air
   I shall never know how they care
      For me, how they care.

And yet I am blest above
All other women, save one,
I am gracious— the pain is gone—
We sit, side by side, at the feast:
How his beauty, my God, is increast
   By the glory of open truth!
He has trusted me with his youth,
Its secrets, its pains, ah rare!
Can he ever know how I care
      For him, how I care?

T0550   An untitled Journal draft in Michael's hand, and surely her work; dated 05
        October 1892, it is a record of the moment (presumably in France that
        June) when Berenson confided his special interest in Mrs Costelloe—
thereby causing consternation to 'the Mikes' and much sick mooning (ZJE 115a) by
Henry. She had a very lucky escape. (Mary incidentally, that May, had suggested
Henry should become a suffragette; on which Henry had tartly pronounced that 'the
cause of womanhood must go hang'. ZJE 100.)

He:	Bernhard Berenson aka "The Doctrine" (ZJE 131a)
beautiful friend:	Mary Costelloe
save one:	presumably Henry, which may explain the following verse
gracious:	ICT would love to have been a fly on the wall.
feast:	possibly *Duval's*, a Paris restaurant (ZJE 120b)
beauty:	His prettiness (judging from photographs) is undeniable. And didn't he know it.
youth:	At this point the *savant* is 27, Mary 28, Edith 30 and Michael 45.

Across a gaudy room
    I looked and saw his face,
Beneath the sapless palm-trees, in the gloom
    Of the distressing place,
    Where everyone sat tired,
    Where talk itself grew stale,
Where, as the day began to fail,
No guest had just the power required
To rise and go: I strove with my disgust;
But at the sight of him my eyes were fired
To give one glance, as though they must
Be sociable with what they found of fair
And free and simple in a chamber where
    Life was so base.

    As when a star is lit
    In the dull, evening sky,
Another soon leaps out to answer it,
    Even so the bright reply
    Came sudden from his eyes,
    By all but me unseen;
Since then the distance that between
    Our lives unalterably lies
Is but a darkness, intimate and still,
Which messages may traverse, where replies
    May sparkle from afar, until
The night becomes a mystery made clear
Between two souls forbidden to draw near:
    Creator, why?

T0554   No surviving autograph has been traced, but assuming the author to be
Henry and the man Berenson, this untitled piece was probably written c
1892. It was published UTB 88-9. If both poems have been correctly
interpreted, it is particularly interesting to compare this piece with *Marionettes* T0638,
in which the protagonists meet again 'after a year'.

gaudy room: This may have been Louise Chandler Moulton's. Henry and Michael
probably first clapped adoring eyes on Berenson in June 1890.
Michael later recalled in a letter to Frances Bradley Brooks 'it was in
her rooms at Paris we first saw Bernhard' (OCX 46o).

A strange sunset

"Oh, my Dear !"
Outside the gates of a mountain town
(The rain was bright on the hawthorn sprays)
Through a wide, gray sky the sun went down,
Spreading tremulous rays,
As a woman's cry broke on my ear,
      "Oh, my Dear !"

      "Oh, my Dear !"
"What is it?" "The light that chanced to suit
Your face as it turned this way. Forgive !"
Her voice was formal, her gaze grew mute:
She may have years to live,
This woman whose passion broke so clear,
      "Oh, my Dear !"

T0596   Multiple drafts of this autograph occur in travel notebooks for their Italian
        trip of 1893 (OYM 48,OYL 11-2); Michael recopied it several times in
        other books, with a footnote *Perugia April 30th*. There was no title until its
final copying (OVM 43b), when an index records the deleted original *A rare sunset*.
Even so slight a piece as this has an eerie quality beyond mere occasional verse;
Michael's woman, unlike Cornford's Fat Lady, does not seem to miss much. Neither
did Michael herself.

T0605   A single draft in the Journal in Michael's hand dated 15 January 1894 (ZJG
        6a), records the momentous first meeting with 'The Painters' (Charles
        Ricketts and Charles Shannon). In the London fog of a late winter afternoon
Will Rothenstein took 'The Poets' to visit them in their studio in Chelsea; the door was
opened by the 30 year old Shannon, whose youthful beauty startled and enraptured
both the susceptible ladies ("Oh, my Dear!"). It all went in the Journal; but it was the
friendship with Ricketts that changed their lives. According to a letter to John Miller
Gray 'The beginning was they sent us a copy of *The Dial*. Then Rothenstein took us
.. to The Vale' (M ZCD 201-3 sa FCR iii). Michael wrote in the Journal 'It is Whistler's
old house..As I am struggling to unmuffle from my furs and wraps, the door is
opened, & an angel— just fresh from "preening", one would say, stands on the
sill...Fairer apparition have I never seen. My heart beat approvingly as I ascended
the stairs' (ZJG 4a). Henry, having compared Shannon to 'a perfect Umbrian
Gabriel, who only wants his lily-stem on his shoulder', continued 'Ricketts is an
unaurioled, decadent Christ, who talks fluently with a mere rill of a voice. One has to

Compensation

Can one wholly wish that the fog should go?
Its furnace-flames through a smoke of snow
Have an opaqueness all their own
As of darkness become a living stone
Of solid impenetrable hue:
There is no mist it is like unto.
It is very flesh of the very flesh
Of a yellow drain, & the tawny mesh,
In place of the gray, & brown, & white,
With a spray of sun, that is London's light,
Has clogged the street with a deep stage gloom
Through wh, if a young face chance to bloom
With its rare, damp rose, you have seen a thing
Most worthy a poet's chronicling.
Such magical pleasures lie to hand
In the jewel-heart of this demon-land!

I had crossed a garden, & someone beat
On what memory called a door, a sheet
Of tarnished orange that straight gave way
And a creature stood on the sill, so gay
In youth & freshness, I could have danced
For joy of the vision the fog enhanced.
The face had a glory of its own
Set in the block of that fulvid stone;
The eyes borrowed nothing from breeze or ray;
They were blue,— more blue the sweet Irish way
As they smiled, & the light on the cheek was keen
As winter-light where the stars have been.
Can one wholly wish that the fog should go?

be on one's rarest behaviour— for nothing ordinary is expected; & a false tone
might be an outrage.' (ZJG 13b). Michael was happy to let Ricketts do the talking:
'One does not ask speech of Shannon. It is enough to see him moving about with
the tea-tray, simple & serviceable...' (ZJG 4a).

fog: The final question mark, overlooked in a second draft, has been restored.
clogged: This line has signs of Henry's emendations; and it was possibly she who
split the text in two stanzas.

Something of Surrey

What I see from the window where I write,
You question. Little to ensnare!—
Tree-tops all of a garden height,
Shadows, and finger-tips, and spears:—
A spike of holly, the flat, blank light
Of a hazel-bower, the shining tiers
Of the deodara, then a pear
Growing bronze in the sun; at last the free
Grace and spread of a forest-tree,
An ash by the outline, and one reaches,
Passing a quarry's knot of fir,
And patch of dotted juniper,
The down, on its ridge a grove of beeches;
And against their bristling curve, and away
Over ranges of hilly croft
  The blue and gray
  Of a sky as soft
As England can make on a summer day.

T0642 An occasional piece which is probably the work of Michael, perhaps in
answer to a letter; the questioner is not known. It was written 29th July
1894. Both autographs are in Michael's hand, with a footnote *10th
Sunday after Trinity* (ZJG 99b,OVO 22b).

Surrey: The poem had a 'Catalogue' title *From my Window* in the Oxford
manuscript (OVO 57b), but the given title persisted into typescript in a
folder labelled *Wild Honey* (OVM 27b). However the piece was never
printed, in WILD HONEY itself, or elsewhere, until now. sa ZJD 18b

deodara: Probably the Himalayan Cedar, (*Cedrus deodara*). Commonly known as
the deodar, it has horizontal, slightly drooping branches.

T0662 This poem was written by Michael on Thursday morning, 29 November
1894 (OVV 60b); the circumstances are evident. It has survived in the
original draft (ZJG 135b) and there are three Oxford manuscripts (one
typed, OVM 38b). In October 1895 the *Atlantic Monthly* published it (JAM
#76,545/OYV 62 sa ZJH 29,ZJJ 4a), and it appeared in Sturge Moore's selection
(SMF 47); Roy Fuller included it in his broadcast appreciation (BBC Radio 3, 03 June
1980), but only Jennifer Breen (ABR, 1994) has reprinted it. Yet this magical poem
lies at the very heart of the Michael Field *oeuvre*.

Second Thoughts

I thought of leaving her for a day
In town, it was such iron winter
At Durdans, the garden frosty clay,
The woods as dry as any splinter,
The sky congested. I would break
From the deep, lethargic, country air
To the shining lamps, to the clash of the play,
And, to-morrow, wake
Beside her, a thousand things to say.
I planned— O more— I had almost started;—
I lifted her face in my hands to kiss,—
A face in a border of fox's fur,
For the bitter black wind had stricken her,
And she wore it— her soft hair straying out
Where it buttoned against the gray, leather snout:
In an instant we should have parted;
But at sight of the delicate world within
That fox-fur collar, from brow to chin,
At sight of those wonderful eyes from the mine,
Coal pupils, an iris of glittering spa,
And the wild, ironic, defiant shine
As of a creature behind a bar
One has captured, and, when three lives are past,
May hope to reach the heart of at last,
All that, and the love at her lips, combined
To show me what folly it were to miss
A face with such thousand things to say,
And beside these, such thousand more to spare,
For the shining lamps, for the clash of the play—
O madness; not for a single day
Could I leave her! I stayed behind.

for a day: The original draft has *just for a day*; there are other minor divergences
from the printed text, including *when* for *but* v17, *them* for *these* v28.
three lives: This is a puzzle: in a reincarnation sense of three *consecutive* lives it will
pass, but Michael is surely referring to two other people, presumably
family. One is obviously Henry herself; the other may be James, as
Amy was always peripheral; if Michael excludes herself, both are
candidates. Francis, Berenson, Ricketts would seem remotely unlikely.

55

I love you with my life— 'tis so I love you;
    I give you as a ring
The cycle of my days till death:
    I worship with the breath
That keeps me in the world with you and spring:
And God may dwell behind, but not above you.

Mine, in the dark, before the world's beginning:
    The claim of every sense,
    Secret and source of every need;
    The goal to which I speed,
And at my heart a vigour more immense
Than will itself to urge me to its winning.

T0678   Written by Henry sometime in February 1895 (ZJH 16b) and copied out by
Michael at least twice (OVJ 122,OVL 36b); in 'The Narrow Book' it appears
as the first of a group of *Winter Lyrics* (OVN 19b). It was published in
WILD HONEY with no title (WDH 71) but listed in the contents as *I love you with my
Life*; Sturge Moore followed this precedent, and justified every verse to the left (SMF
49). This is arguably the finest of all the Michael Field love-lyrics; it is almost with
incredulity that one realises the subject of such devotion is the dreadful 'Bernie'. As
ever, when the chthonic hormones bubble up in the basement the critical faculty
abseils from the attic. Yet the evidence is incontrovertible: in December 1907 Henry
recalled in the Journal 'I have written to Bernhard in the old years— And God may
be behind but not above you' (ZJX 56ab). This was the time when her infatuation
with Berenson was at its peak. Henry poured out her emotions in the 1895 Journal in
a series of extravagant and unfortunate pieces (T0676-7;9-80,2,4-6); how many of
us have not, in the grip of the Stranger, been equally intemperate? But amongst
them was this pearl, which might almost have been written by 'the Portuguese'.
Edwin Essex described it as 'pre-eminent' and as 'a superb love-poem' (JCM 236).

The goal: Angela Leighton, writing much sense about the love poetry, remarks 'In
the place of sentimentalism, Michael Field offers a kind of literal,
elemental Darwinism of the heart' (FAL 233). She can be forgiven for
apparently not suspecting the unworthy focus of this particular poem.

56

Pen-prints

Ah me, how I wish the summer back,
Or wish we were creatures underground,
I am horribly dismal; for the snow
Makes the world opaque, & the only sound
I hear is the gardener sweeping
The garden path; but no!
A pen at my right is keeping
On its imperturbable, wavy track—
I smile, nor pray for the summer back,
Since happiness that has no stint
Is mine, as long as that even flow
Continues, as long as I catch a hint
On the page of her spirit's pattering print.

Neither Berenson nor Mary could be persuaded to take the Michael Field closet dramas seriously (VMS 124-5), and this was eventually to resolve the problem. In November they were sent a copy of the latest— ATTILA, MY ATTILA!— and received it 'with jeers and uncontrollable laughter... our friendship closes'. The insult to the playwrights was unforgivable; the breach was to last seven years. Henry wrote in the Journal 'My womanhood is dying' (ZJJ 28b). But in her usual end-of-year summary she salvaged some of her wounded pride: 'I love him inexorably by fate— as I give him up by choice' (ZJJ 55a)

T0695   Two autographs have survived, both in Michael's hand. The first in a tall 'Narrow Book' is undated, but bracketed within poems known to be written in February 1895 (OVN 6b); this seems to be a reasonable date for *Pen-prints* as well. The second 'fair' copy is in *Perpetua*, the notebook of poems specifically written about Henry (OVV 56b). This has the footnote date *1896*, almost certainly an error; chronology in the later stages of this notebook is erratic. In these lines we have a rare sight of 'the twain' at their literary labours. Henry was to record a similar moment at Richmond some 16 years later, noting she could 'hear the sound of my Loved One's breath as I write; we can speak during an interim of writing' (ZKB 87a).

snow: There is here, at least, tenuous corroboration of the season.

57

Meeting the Sea

Amaze,
And strife at the heart! Shall I join the clods,
Mere breathers of brine, who pace for days
This triple promenade beneath the rods
Of tamarisk, fretting the blue sky-line
On the cliff with fibres of sappy red,
Or, more enduring, take a seat
And stare for hours at the wavering sheet—
Men with faith in a perfect cure,
For the wind is strong, & the air is pure,
And the motto for delicate lungs,— Endure!
Oh, leave them, leave them their barren walk,
Their pier, their "shelters", & chief their view
Of flagstones cutting the fluid blue,—
And down with me to the soaking chalk,
    Down to a sea that's suddy,
To sands one must run on with naked feet,
To— what is that orange spot? The gracious
Moist, deliciously vivacious
Shine of the periwinkle shell,
Golden burnish on the muddy
Oozing reefs. How all is well
'Mid these suave low contours. There is no colour
Over the sea: the dance of rays,
Halfway twixt the tide marks & the verge,
Is growing every instant duller;
And, as I stoop to give a twist
To my crocus shell, sea & air combine,
And we look on, into the opaline
    Region of wide, sea-mist. . .
    A stake.
Felt in its iron grip of sand,
And, for the rest, irrelevant,
Evasive light of one woof with the sky:
Now there is neither far nor nigh;
For the sea is sunk to a frothy lip,
Twilight blot & smoke of a ship
Are struck on the air high overhead:
And somewhere, deep in the brine, the surge

Is softening its low hiss to a hum
Like an exile, I pace the scant
Open beach by the frothy scum,
And muse on the mysteries that are
Beyond the penetrable bar
Wrapt in the cloud of that rhythmic land:
Desiring to lie on the silver strand
Of its wonderful, central, silver lake,
With prairies of silver-shore,
Where no echo can ever come,
Where nothing can ever steal on the sight:—
Gold & silver & shaded light
   For ever & evermore,
And, on the ear, the infinite,
Muted memory of the reach
Of waves that strain against a shingly beach.

T0700   In March 1895 they were at Eastbourne. In the Journal for Friday 15th
Henry recorded 'This morning we rambled toward Beachy Head on the
shore, staining our dresses with chalk-slime & enjoying those little amber
pebbles, alive with a beast inside them— the sea-periwinkles, that here & there lay
moist on the sand, deliciously vivacious..'(ZJH 29a). Michael worked at drafts of a
narrative poem which incorporated several phrases taken direct from Henry's prose;
a late version, still unpolished but with splendid drive, is reproduced here (ZJH 32-5).
The same text, also in Michael's hand, appears in an Oxford manuscript (OVN 9b).
On the Saturday Henry succumbed to toothache, which may account for the sour
note of the next entry: 'Eastbourne is a hateful place— The ocean besieged by 3
Parades— the terraces stiff & gray without being noble as at Brighton— the newest
red part diffuse & irrationally gabled. It is windy, fatiguing...' And there is a delightful
vignette: 'a Boarding House gives us the feeling of being at an asylum. One poor
governess, sensitive, lonely, neurotic, clung to us touchingly, & seemed the better for
our smiles. She had lost all whom she loved in two years, & twice the news of death
had come by telegram—'(ZJH 31a). Michael was to return to a sea theme (T0872).

suddy: 'The Sea strikes me this year as something so soft— almost "suddy"-— It
            fills one's eyes... with an infinite suavity' (H ZJH 29a).
tamarisk: A feathery shrub, *T. anglica*, planted and seaside naturalized; it has
            spikelike racemes of pink flowers.
periwinkle: Almost certainly the flat periwinkle *Littorina mariae* (?*fabali*s 1825),
            yellow or orange/red; less probably its close relative *L. obtusata* which
            can be yellow, but is normally olive-green or striated brown.
stake: This reference is a little clearer in a variant text at v31:
                How all is altered, half-opaque,
                Luminous, magic,— one jutting stake
                Beside me, felt in its iron grip
                Of the sand, the rest irrelevant.   (ZJH 32b)

(Chorus of Nymphs of Artemis Dictynna)

Hither, fellows of the chase,
Hither with the dry, bent bow,
Hither with the buskin, hither
With the chiton to the knee
And inviolable zone,
With the fillet at the temples,
Breast untamed, and crystal voice
Ringing through the forest-brakes,
Ringing through the western breezes,
Mingled with the horn that echoes
And the pressure of the streams.

Come to prove your maiden zest,
Prove your own pure liberty,
Ye whose spirits have no lord,
Ye whose every sense is chill
With the freshness of its birth;
Ye secure from any feeling
That can visit as a doom;
Ye who live and hunt as men,
Ye who do not burn as they—
Women in your pride and yet
Never is the glory yielded;
Ye who share with mortals solely
What is yokeless in their state,
Sovereign each within yourselves!

T0763 During April 1896 they visited Devon, an experience that prompted Henry
to attempt a masque 'like *Comus*' (ZJK 62a,ZJN 106a). This was to be
NOONTIDE BRANCHES *A small sylvan drama interspersed with songs and
invocations* and by late July it was complete, 'our equal care' (H ZJK 85b). Oxford
has a pair of manuscripts, one in each hand (OQY,OQZ). The scene is set in 'A
Woodland by a tidal river in the West of England', where Artemis enters 'with her
Nymphs': this is their response to her command to *Sound your call, /And bid your
sister-huntresses approach* (XNB 2-3). The chorus is probably Henry's work. She
wrote in the Journal for Whitsunday (May 24) "I begin the Masque— The prologue of
Artemis" (ZJK 90a); she had a special interest in "that unrhymed form" (ZJK 196a).

Artemis Dictynna: Dictynna, a goddess of sailors and hunters, was originally

Good Friday

There is wild shower and winter on the main.
Foreign and hostile, as the flood of Styx,
The rumbling water: and the clouds that mix
And drop across the land, and drive again
Whelm as they pass. And yet the bitter rain,
The fierce exclusion hurt me not; I fix
My thought on the deep-blooded crucifix
My lips adore, and there is no more pain.
A Power is with me that can love, can die,
That loves, and is deserted, and abides;
A loninesss that craves me and enthrals:
And I am one with that extremity,
One with that strength. I hear the alien tides
No more, no more the universe appals.

Britomartis (sa T1089), one of the Nymphs of Artemis until herself deified
by Artemis; in Sparta the two were worshipped as one deity. For a character
of Artemis see footnote to T0321.

buskin: Probably a calf or knee length boot; the *kothornos* of the tragedians seems
less practical.

chiton: See footnote to T0357

zone: A girdle or belt.

fillet: A band for the hair, presumably to avoid Absalomian entanglements during
maidenly galumphings through the thickets.

T0800 This poem was written by Michael 16-8 April 1897 during their stay at Lyme
Regis. She wrote in the Journal (for 'Holy Saturday') "Last night I went alone
to the sea-marge. There was rain..." (ZJL 41b). The first draft follows on ZJL
43b; there are three other Oxford autographs, one a fair copy by Henry (OVL 21b).
Ten years later Henry recalled "Michael wrote a noble sonnet, bleak as a stripped
altar" (ZJW 54b). It was eventually published in WILD HONEY as the last poem in
the book (WDH 194). One of the very finest of Michael's sonnets, one feels it was
shortsighted of Ricketts to view it with disfavour— actual 'dislike' and 'distaste' (ZJY
9a). "He refers to the last poems as imprudent" (H ZJY 46a). Here is no religioso
tosh. However intellectually destitute the christian placebo, one cannot but admire
and be moved by the active intellect engaged with it, in such memorable images.

Styx: The 'hateful' river bounding Tartarus on the Western side; here Charon plies
his ferry, see T1060.

love: The Journal draft has *bow* (v9); there are also interesting *varia* for v12-4.

The Torrent

And here thy footsteps stopped? This writhing swell,
This surging, mad, voluminous, white stream,
Burst starving from the hills, knows what befell
That instant in the clear midsummer beam?
To me in the grey, azure iris-bed
Of the old garden, I was left to tend,
And tended, came the word that thou wert dead . . .
Is it on these round eddies I must spend
My passionate conjecture? Thou art gone;
And I am brought to these orchestral shores,
This clanging music, where I dare not moan,
Dare not lament! Fountain from fountain pours—
Yea, they have borne thee, yea, they bear thee on
To the smooth-rushing waters of the Rhone.

T0804   On 12 June 1897, James Cooper, Edith's 79-year-old father, left with his
younger daughter Amy on a fateful visit to Switzerland. She was never
again to see him alive; in Zermatt on the 24th he went out alone for a
walk one evening, and disappeared. Correspondence in *The Times* followed the
mystery, and the famous mountaineer of the Matterhorn, Edward Whymper, wrote to
Henry with kindly and informed advice (ZCF 231-45). On the 9th of July Michael
Field went to the Riffelalp in person, pursuing fruitless enquires for three weeks (ZJL
82-99). By late August the puzzle seemed insoluble, and it was assumed his body
had fallen into water and been swept downstream. On Friday 03 September Michael
began what was to become a great cycle of sonnets on the theme, with this
quatorzain. It was originally titled *The viewless fields* (ZJL 107b), then this title was
used, (at least up to December, when Henry wrote 'The Viewless Fields of Michael
have grown mightily' ZJL 163b) as a heading for the entire cycle. It is a quotation
from Sophocles' *Oedipus at Colonus*: 'he was snatched to the viewless fields by
some swift, strange doom' (M ZJL 101a); Henry had written of her father "He was to
me as Oedipus to Antigone" (ZJL 79-80). At some unknown date, perhaps as late as
31 October 1898 (OVQ 57b), the cycle became *The Longer Allegiance*, a phrase
also from Sophocles, this time from *Antigone*, 'for I owe a longer allegiance to the
dead than to the living: in that world I shall abide for ever' (M OVQ 17b). At this
time Michael copied out the sonnets into a new notebook (OVR) with this epigraph,
and *The Torrent* (OVQ 18b), which had been #1 in the sequence, was briefly
displaced by *Elect* (T0859). This sonnet was later suppressed, and *The Torrent* was
once again to open the cycle in WILD HONEY (WDH 137).

grey: In the Journal draft (also YSL 2.9), this is *long*, which perhaps had best
been left; *grey* precedes *azure* not over-comfortably.

62

Oxford

Dear city, not for what thou wert of yore
I love thee— for the blotting shades of yew
On thy rare lawns, the rich sweep of the dew
Crystal between the mulberry-berried floor,
The fig-leaf-dropping path; by one low door
The grape-vine with its clustering bunches blue,
And violet, dull leaves; the one or two
Pears ripening round the gargoyles, or before
Thy blackened halls. Thy charm is in the air
And haunts it as a ghost: the balsam scent
And withering of thy flowers is as elsewhere
In autumn meadow-lands it cannot be:
So much fair hope, so many summers spent—
'Tis Nature with the ruth of history.

old garden: James had been a farmer, and was still a keen gardener.
dare not: Michael was excessively protective of her niece, assuming the slightest
shock might be fatal (OCL 42); Henry played up to this, as part of her
attention-seeking personal *mystique*. The reality was, she was tough as
old boots; one has only to consider the stoicism with which she bore
her last dreadful years of illness. Michael paid the price in stress.

T0808 By 09 September, with the matter of James still unresolved, they were in
Oxford; it is likely they were staying at 15 Turl Street (OCX 93o)— 'Our
beloved Turl rooms under the blackness of Lincoln's frown' (H ZJL 121a). It
is certain that they visited Exeter College (v.i.). In October Michael wrote to her cousin
Frances ('Fanny') Brooks "I have written 2 sonnets in Oxford" (OCX 175o): in fact she
accomplished four, this one and T0805,6/7,9. The Journal draft for *Oxford* is dated
precisely Wednesday 13 October 1897 (ZJL 129b). For a time the sonnet was in
The Longer Allegiance set (OVR 7b); in WILD HONEY it was placed in the group
titled *Mane et Vespere*, *ICT:* 'Morning and Evening' (WDH 113).

yew: Perhaps Merton garden, with 'its lime-walk, its old yew-hedge' (ZJL 121b)
between: One draft (YSL 2.9) has *across*, also *branches* for *bunches* in v6.
fig: Exeter: 'In the garden the memorable sight is the old wall covered with
fig-trees' (H ZJL 122a,3a). The *grape-vine* of v6 was at St. John's (122b).
the air: 'The melancholy of Oxford....comes from walls & from the air....'
balsam: '.... we walked the gardens of Corpus, smelt the balsams' (H ZJL 122b).
ruth: sorrow, regret.

Being Free

Belovèd, I shall speak of thee no more:
It is thy freedom now that thou art dead.
By speech we are not bound as heretofore,
For thou dost come the way that God doth tread,
Through the great solitudes that lovers use:
With spring and star-break, where deep music is,
After long, lashing storms we interfuse,
And Life requires no more that Lachesis
Sing to her of the Past. Nay, we are free,
Profuse, delicious, giving each to each
Love that we dared not give to memory
To be the guardian of, or trust to speech,
The kindling certitude of lip or eye:
Love one can only taste, Death standing by.

T0824   James's body was discovered by woodmen on the 25th October; according
to a newspaper report 'He lay as one asleep, his right arm under his face'
(ZJL 133a). He was buried at Zermatt on the 30th. After attending the
burial, and a stopover at Montreux, Michael Field was back in England by 13
November (ZJL 135-45); the sonnet cycle grew with a renewed vigour, and this
english sonnet is unequivocally dated Wednesday 15 December 1897. All three
known autographs are in Michael's hand; in the "First Version of The Longer
Allegiance" it bears two trial titles, *In Death's Sight* (OVQ 29b), and, in an Index,
Death being Witness. The final title *Being Free* appears with the fair copy version
OVR 15b. Curiously, when published in WILD HONEY, this sonnet was removed
from *The Longer Allegiance* cycle, and appears in a separate group of pieces (WDH
123). This has the effect of making the *Belovèd* an anonymous, universal figure,
rather than a specific, immediately identifiable one; perhaps, given the tone of the
poem, and the person, this was thought more appropriate. (This is probably the
reason why *Elect* , almost identical in theme, was suppressed altogether.)

no more: Not strictly true; the sonnet cycle had some way to run, and Michael was
still writing about James with a genuine affection in 1901 (T0987).

Lachesis: One of the three Moerae (the Fates) who decide destiny, and length of
life. *Clotho* spins the linen thread of a man's life and *Lachesis* measures
it with her rod; the fearsome *Atropos* eventually cuts it with her shears.

Past: The Moerae are similar to the Norns of Scandinavia, and here Lachesis
is assuming some of the character of Urd.

(Song)

I would not have the wind pass by
   I would not have it rave,
I would not have the wind draw nigh
   That whistled o'er his grave.

I would not have the rain beat round,
   I would not hear the rain;
There is no comfort in the sound,
   No comfort for us twain.

But I would have the snow drift high,
   And to my house-roof cling,
So for a night at least we lie
   Beneath one covering.

delicious: sharing enjoyment

only taste: As often, the Scottish autograph YSL 2.9 is variant; at this point it reads *taste alone*. The deleted titles of OVQ emphasised the theme of the poem more precisely— that mortality allows only a limited experience of love.

T0826   This apparently effortless lyric is almost certainly Michael's; both autographs are in her hand, with the footnote *Christmas Eve 1897* (OVQ 39b,OVR 96b). A few days before she had written a closely related poem T0825, in which the tempest *Threw o'er the summer's corse a sheet of snow*, so it seems Durdans was indeed under snow. The lyric was added as one of the new poems in the final (American) edition of UNDERNEATH THE BOUGH, published by Thomas Mosher of Portland ME in October 1898 (UTD 32).

his grave: Whose grave is involved cannot be in doubt, even if not borne out by manuscript context; T0825 also refers to *torrents* and *faded dead*.

In January 1898 the 3-month old puppy Whym Chow (named for Edward *Whym*per) will arrive; he becomes their constant companion. The next eight years are to be the happiest and most carefree of their lives.

Fifty Quatrains

'Twas fifty quatrains: and from unknown strands
The Woman came who sang them on the floor.
I saw her, I was leaning by the door,
—Saw her strange raiment and her lovely hands;
And saw . . . but that I think she sang— the bands
Of low-voiced women on a happy shore:
Incomparable was the haze, and bore
The many blossoms of soft orchard lands.
'Twas fifty quatrains, for I caught the measure;
And all the royal house was full of kings,
Who listened and beheld her and were dumb;
Nor dared to seize the marvellous rich pleasure,
Too fearful even to ask in whisperings,
The ramparts being closed, whence she had come.

T0862   In late 1898 'Michael sent the Artists each a sonnet' (H ZJM 138a). These
were T0861 *A Train of Queens*, which was for Shannon, and the present
T0862 *Fifty Quatrains*, 'dedicated to' Ricketts. The poems are extraordinary,
seemingly ideal subject matter for paintings, and were later published side by side in
WILD HONEY, WDH 40-1. Here Michael Field was writing, as Margaret Sackville so
memorably described it, 'verse like metal beaten into all manner of glittering shapes'
(AMS xx); this is the world of Dante Gabriel Rossetti's *blesséd damozel*, of
Burne-Jones's *The Wheel of Fortune*, and *The Golden Stairs* (he had died that June).
Yet apparently its source was in Michael's "Irish stuff" (M ZJM 134b), and the Irish
background is certainly evident in T0861, with the direct reference to Cuchulain. The
"Irish stuff" was the new play DEIRDRE which was engaging them at the time. *Fifty
Quatrains* is much the better of the two sonnets, and deservedly has been widely
anthologized. Henry refers to 'that woman seen alone in the vision of her by the
page at the door' (ZJM 134b), but there is no other clue as to who she might be.
The two Oxford autographs, both in Michael's hand, are undated (OVU 20b,OWG
24b), but her original 1898 Journal draft has the footnote *Wednesday 21 December*
(ZJM 132b). The Artists were now living in Richmond, and the following January
Ricketts was to suggest Michael Field should move there too; then Shannon found
them an idyllic little house by the river. As the old year died Amy became engaged
to John Ryan (25 December 1898). The days at Durdans were drawing to a close.

quatrains: poetic stanzas of four verses
that: Sturge Moore italicises this word (SMF 62)
happy shore: It is remotely possible there is a looking back here to LONG AGO,
                 and Sappho's island.

Old Age

Was it at ebb or flow, that water wide
Soaked in dark sands, between the banks of Dee,
So still it stood, I questioned presently
A bowed old man at work by the roadside.
"The tides are high in Springtime," he replied.
"Yes, yes, but now," I pressed impatiently—
He looked across then shook his head— "I see
The water, but I cannot see the tide."
O block of age, O sorrow, broken glass!
O deafness to the trembling hand of time!
Were it not better to be wholly blind
Than miss the sweet, frail moments as they pass,
The shadow of the wavelets fain to climb,
The little mounds of sand they leave behind.

T0874   Known only from a draft (ZJN 39b) and a fair copy (OVU 23b), this
        unpublished piece was written by Michael 05 March 1899, and based on
        an anecdote she recorded in the Journal (ZJN 38b). At the time they were
having a brief holiday at Parkgate, Deeside. Michael had written a few days earlier
another italian sonnet on the ebbtide (T0873). That one was pure magic, one of so
very many: to her, writing a sonnet came as naturally as breathing. Here she may be
seen writing just for the fun of it.

presently: the peremptory Shaksperian 'at once'.
block of age: One has some sympathy with the maligned ancient on Dee sands,
                whose peasant wit is regrettably lost on Michael. He possibly took an
                uncharitable view of this imperious, well-dressed Mary with time on
                her gloved hands, and her cattle still not called home.
glass: most probably *hour*-glass rather than a mirror, with a further echo in
                the final verse.
mounds: The draft text offers an earlier version of this last verse (in part
                discarded, perhaps, for the sake of the Time conceit):

                        And their sand-dimpled foot-prints left behind

67

Nests in Elms

The rooks are cawing up and down the trees!
Among their nests they caw. O sound I treasure,
Ripe as old music is, the summer's measure,
Sleep at her gossip, sylvan mysteries,
With prate and clamour to give zest of these—
In rune I trace the ancient law of pleasure,
Of love, of all the busy-ness of leisure,
With dream on dream of never-thwarted ease.
O homely birds, whose cry is harbinger
Of nothing sad, who know not anything
Of sea-birds' loneliness, of Procne's strife,
Rock round me when I die! So sweet it were
To die by open doors, with you on wing
Humming the deep security of life.

T0878 One of Michael's nature poems; many drafts exist, all in her hand. The
date of the final version is 17 March 1899 (OWG 21b,OVR 39b). These
were the last days at Reigate before the momentous removal to Richmond:
'Just as we are getting ready to leave Durdans the rooks settle in the elms beyond
our garden' (M ZJN 47a). For a while the poem was included in the sonnet sequence
The Longer Allegiance (sa OVQ 62b), but its superfluousness in this context was
realised when the poem was eventually published in WILD HONEY, WDH 62. Henry
(probably) had much earlier written a fey poem about rooks, T0593; and Michael
was to return to the subject, in an equally slight piece, the following February, T0904.

Among their nests:	Sturge Moore published a mutilated version of the poem which omitted this verse, and verses 4-6 (SMF 72).
law of pleasure:	Angela Leighton has made a discerning analysis, and points to an echo in Charlotte Mew's *Afternoon Tea* (FAL 239,95).
Procne:	Sister of Philomela. When her husband Tereus raped Philomela and then cut out Procne's tongue, Procne cooked their young son Itys and served him up to his father with two veg. The sisters then flew off, Procne as a swallow and Philomela as a nightingale, hotly pursued by Tereus as a hoopoe (or perhaps a hawk). Michael Field wrote further on these unlikely avian shenanigans in *Sonata Philomela* T0983-5; sa T0314.
Rock round me:	'I should like to die to the cawing of the rooks. It is such a wise sound' (M ZJO 164b).

Nightfall

She sits beside: through four low panes of glass
The sun, a misty meadow, and the stream;
Falling through rounded elms the last sunbeam.
Through night's thick fibre sudden barges pass
With great forelights of gold, with trailing mass
Of timber: rearward of their transient gleam
The shadows settle, and profounder dream
Enters, fulfils the shadows. Vale and grass
Are now no more; a last leaf strays about,
Then every wandering ceases; we remain.
Clear dusk, the face of wind is on the sky:
The eyes I love lift to the upper pane—
Their voice gives note of welcome quietly
"I love the air in which the stars come out".

T0893   This italian sonnet has survived in at least five autographs, all in Michael's
        hand and obviously her work. It was completed 16 October 1899 (ZJN
        111a,YFB 8b) though the original inspiration seems to have been an
        evening five days previously; they had now been living at 1, The Paragon some five
        months. (Amy and John had married from the new home on 25 September and for
        a while would live at Clifton, where they had probably first met). The view of the
        Thames consoled even in the last dark days. Michael wrote in the Journal, Nov/Dec
        1911 'So often we have sat together— looking across to those trees & barges in the
        mist' (ZKB 153a). As with several others, this poem was originally included in the
        sonnet sequence The Longer Allegiance (OVR 47b,OVQ 70b) until the judicious
        pruning for publication in WILD HONEY, WDH 171.

She sits beside: Probably in the 'Sun Room' (ZKA 57b), but conceivably in
                   Michael's study, her 'green room' (ZJO 134b) that was to
                   become the 'Gold Room' (ZJY 85a), below it . Sturge Moore left
                   a description of Paragon (WAD xvii-xviii, sa OYS 15o).
The eyes I love: This verse retains a faint echo of an early sketch (OVU 43a) for
                   the opening lines of the sonnet:

                           I think we watch together with the eyes
                           That one day shall see God— look on the stream

I love the air: "'I like the air when the stars come out' Love says, & then our
                   spirits close up together" (M ZJN 110b).

69

The Old Hundred Years

God, Thou art gathering in Thy bosom's fold
The hundred years where all I love drew breath,
And sought and found their little age of gold,
And fell on dreams awhile, then fell on death.
Oh, sweet the summers that have known their prime,
The English hedgerows where the catkins blew
When they were passing by or breathed the time
Of the roses red and white and all their dew!
Oh, blest to them the earth, to them the sky!
But now, of human kind, one only hears
How ran their accents when great news befell
Or how they listened when the lark sang high:
Gone are those days of simple miracle:
Thou coverest their voices with the years.

T0897 Luckily this poem can be consulted in its early draft and two other
autographs, for the published versions are both incorrect. It was written
31 December 1899, almost certainly by Michael, who, according to
Henry, had 'done some dozen good sonnets' (ZJN 143a). It was however based on
Henry's Journal note: 'It is terribly moving to leave our great & beloved Dead in
their Century— it seems as if Time laid over them another Coffin-lid' (ZJN 142b).
Originally another of the sequence *The Longer Allegiance* (OVQ 73b,OVR 50b), the
quatorzain unaccountably lost its twelfth verse when published in WILD HONEY,
WDH 162, as well as suffering a typographic error in verse five.

Hundred Years:	In the original draft (ZJN 144b), it was titled *On the last night of the nineteenth Century*. This of course is patently incorrect, as they later realised ('Michael will be discovered in the 20th Century' H ZJO 180a). The mistake however has returned, bolder than ever, in contemporary vapourings of the ignorant and innumerate anent 01 January 2000 as the "first day of the new Millenium".
prime:	This appears in WILD HONEY as *praise;* Sturge Moore corrected the (?printer's) error in his selection from the poems (SMF 115)
Or how they:	And also replaced the missing verse 12; but, irritatingly, could not resist tinkering with it, and inserting it after verse 9 instead of in its correct place after verse 11.

That December saw the fall of at least one significant coffin-lid. Mary Costelloe's
husband had died on the 20th, leaving the way open for her marriage to Bernhard
Berenson the following year (29 December 1900). For Henry the dream was over.

70

Returning

What time the stock-dove found
    That there was tender ground
And trees to mark the measure of her flight,
    With olive leaf in beak
    No longer did she seek
The stranded ark: she flew
  To an elder-bush she knew
    And there did wait
    For troops of doves,
  For the one troop she loves
    To congregate

I would not thus conceive,
    So I might fare
Where those beloved were
    That note on note
    Taught me to brood:
But, with remembrance unsubdued,
  Home through the oozy air
    To one that stood
  Praying the unstable flood
    That it should keep
    Still deathful-deep,
    I should return, & rest,
Assuaging that soft breast,
Until the broken water was forgot,
    Until it mattered not,
    If there were field or flood.

T0903   Two autographs exist, both in Michael's hand, (ZJO 31a,OVX 7b); the
poem was written sometime 18-25 February 1900, 'Within the covers of
last week' (M ZJO 31a). The Deluge metaphor makes one wonder if it had
been a damp month; but the poem is coincidentally a curious pre-echo of T1595.

stock-dove: Michael had likened herself to this bird at least once before (T0266).
ark: There seems little doubt of the historicity of at least one monumental
            inundation, surviving in folk-memory in the arks of Xisuthros,
            Deucalion, and the pretty myth of Noah (Genesis VIII 8-12).

Mintha

Dusk Mintha, purple-eyed, I love thy story—
  Where was the grove,
Beneath what alder-strand, or poplar hoary
Did silent Hades look to thee of love?
Mute wert thou, ever mute, nor did'st thou start
Affrighted from thy doom, but in thy heart
Did'st bury deep thy god. Persephone
Passed thee by slowly on her way to hell;
And seeing Death so sore beloved of thee
She sighed, and not in anger wrought the spell
  Fixed thee a plant
Of low, close blossom, of supprest perfume,
  And leaves that pant
Urgent as if from spices of a tomb.

T0914   Michael wrote this poem in April 1900; one text (OWE 11b) assigns it to
    Low Sunday (the 22nd), but it seems clear from the Journal drafts (ZJO
    52a) it was substantially written earlier in the week. Several autographs
exist, the poem being part of a group *In Persian Gardens*, which Henry described as
'strange, new-moulded' (ZJO 182b). Ricketts was left a copy, and discussed it on his
following visit (ZJO 57b); it was published in WILD HONEY, WDH 11. The tale is that
of the nymph Minthe, seduced by Hades, god of Tartarus (the Underworld). She was
rescued in the sprig of time by Persephone his Queen, who changed the nymph into
a mint plant, thus ensuring everything ended up smelling sweetly.

alder-strand: The alder is a tree symbolic of rebirth, which grew (with black poplar
          and cypress) at the mouth of Calypso's cave. It is also associated
          with Circe, and Orpheus, who returned from Tartarus. When cut, its
          wood turns from white to the purplish-red of shed blood.
poplar hoary: Hades had also attempted the virtue of the nymph Leuce, who was
          similarly transformed to a white poplar (aspen); this tree stands in
          Tartarus by the pool of Memory. White poplar was sacred to
          Persephone as goddess of renewal; Heracles wove himself a wreath
          from its leaves before returning from Tartarus at the end of his
          twelfth Labour. The gate of Tartarus is hidden by black poplars.
spices ...tomb: Mint was one of several aromatic herbs used at funeral ceremonies
          to combat any odours of corruption.

72

Stuffed Birds

Home in my sun-room; but I cannot write;
The glitter of the balsam is too quick,
The shining on the walls too fair a white:
Oh for that forest-room, where, through the thick
Of his glass-case the thoughtful penguin thought,
The kestral-hawk blooded his wren in death,
And the haw-finches on bare boughs besought
Of me the freedom of their dew-dipped breath,
That parrot mouldered in her apple wings,
And beauty dropping! There my heart had play,
I sang with that dulled Nature in my ken;
I sang, I comforted the stricken things,
Gave to the owl her night, the hawk its prey,
A gush of anguish to the deep-clawed wren.

T0936   There are several weird Michael Field poems, but this has to be one of the weirdest; Henry recorded in the Journal 'Michael has written her sonnet to the birds of our parlour at Holmsley cottage' (ZJO 129a). They had been spending their summer in the New Forest, staying in a gamekeeper's lodge, 'There are cases of wild animals in the parlour' (ZJO 63b). Mr Cole's exhibits apparently included an owl, a hawk, a cockatoo and a penguin (ZJO 100b,27b). The piece was written on the return to Paragon; two autographs exist (ZJO 130a, OVX 32b), both dated Sunday 15 (ICT: 16) September 1900. One does wonder about that penguin.

my sun-room: Conceivably Michael's 'green room' (see note to T0893, also T0939); but more likely to be the drawing room above it, if the walls indeed shine 'too fair a white'

balsam: Equally ambiguous; in her own room at that time Michael had 'a pot of balsams' (T0940), but on balance it is probable she is referring to one of Henry's flower arrangements; of the fulvid balsam *I. capensis*, gathered by the Thames, as in the previous September (T0891). And these would be in the drawing room.

Platonic Love

Things seen: of these the poetasters write—
No matter! 'Tis what happens out of sight,
Full six feet below vision, may requite

- The dreary havoc of a London street,
A cackle as of parrots in a rage.
I turn to see— jarred ear & angry feet—
What toy, what wonder may men's minds engage.

- A Punch & Judy show in all the blare
Of its quick-shifted scenes, &, sitting there,
Undisturbed; for he had no part, just then,
No entrance in the whirl of puppet-men,
A small, white terrier-dog was looking forth.
White, & shivering, for the wind blew north.

It was nipping, & no hand there to caress,
No voice: And all the loneliness that clings
From the sorrow of not remembering things
Just craving them, was in the eye askance
That fell on mine, warm, soft to his distress—
Two kingdoms met & greeted in that glance!

The passion— all he had for me in hoard
A stranger, in that one brief glance adored,
All his madness to run far, starve, & die
For me, there as he caught me, passing by!

All that he blindly waited, all he craved
Chidden in that dull life where he behaved,—
To live without a kick, to wag his tail
Unfeignedly, & by sheer bliss prevail:
And the dear being loved again that way
Without the chink of coin, or hire, or pay.

An instant! And there ran across the brain
Of this mute, shivering creature at the show
The torture of an apprehended good.
Whether the hope will come to him again
As he sits up, aloof, I do not know:
But we encountered, but we understood.

T0947   Only known from a draft in the Journal in Michael's hand (ZJO 150b,1b).
The piece is unassigned, but from bracketing dates seems to have been
written 9-10 November 1900. Informal, unrevised, it provides a glimpse of
Michael's ready facility to seize a passing moment and capture it brilliantly; in this
case a cameo of a London street. At the heart of it a sudden empathy with that
sorrow which comes from having no happier time (unlike Aguecheek) to remember,
the torture of an *apprehended* good. Deep stuff for one kerbside mutt.

Platonic Love: Love without sensual desire, in this context removed even further from
its original *amor socraticus*.

poetaster: 'A writer of contemptible verses' (Chambers Dictionary). On a visit to
the Lake District and Albert Fleming at the end of August 1893 they
met one such unfortunate, a cleric, whose *chef d'œuvre* was entitled
'Venus' Looking Glass'. "We all roar over the Canon's poem", Mr
Fleming "from the midst of tears" (ZJF 57ab). A few Journal pages
later "the fatal poem is brought out" once again (retitled 'Diana's
looking-glass'). It says much for the good nature of Michael Field
that they did not seem put out by a similar reception for *Bury her at
Even* (ZJF 62ab). By 1910 Henry was almost resigned to the fact that
'being a poet is to be a monster' (ZKA 97b). She was right of course.

cackle: Almost certainly a reference to the showman's *swazzle*, or squeaker—
a mouthed reed made from two convex pieces of metal with a tape
stretched from side to side between them. With this he voiced the
traditional high-pitched buzzing squawk of 'Mr. Punch'.

nipping: cold

Violets

These offered violets are not for regret
That thou can'st never give my bosom ease;
My fond, reservèd tears, if they should wet
Mine eyes, were of far blacker tinct than these.
Nor do I give them with the idle hope
Their stealthy drops thy senses should engage;
The passion at my heart has larger scope,
A bird of sweeping pinion in a cage.
Yet shalt thou grasp the force of my intent,
Pity my doom nor do my pride despite,
Who am as one by a god's fury rent,
Cast to the dust, humbled from all men's sight:
Yea, learn how their nativity empowers—
Sprung from the blood of Ajax are these flowers.

T0948 An english sonnet, one of the *In Persian Gardens* group, written by Michael (ZJO 182b); there are variant drafts of the sestet (ZJO 162a,70a;OWA 48a). Most versions are dated 01 December 1900, and one autograph has the footnote *proved afterwards I think to be the death-day of Oscar Wilde* (OVX 48). Wilde actually died in Paris the previous day, but the curious relevance of verses 8,11-2 is probably fortuitous. Ursula Bridge says the poem was sent with a bouquet to Ricketts (OZM 95), and the poem seems rather to reflect an increasing involvement with 'the Painter'. It was published in WILD HONEY, WDH 16.

sweeping pinion:	The Greek name of Ajax, *Aias*, derives from *Aietos*, the eagle of Zeus. This appeared to Telamon at the request of Heracles, to confirm the future bravery of his newborn son.
a god's fury:	Ajax angered the goddess Athene by his boastfulness. She struck him mad, so that he slaughtered a herd of cattle and sheep in mistake for the Trojan foe, and then killed himself.
blood of Ajax:	In August, Michael recorded she had read that 'violets are sprung from the blood of Ajax' (ZJO 101b); but those flowers were probably larkspur, which are marked *AI*, the first two letters of his Greek name (also a cry of woe). Violets are usually associated with the shed blood of the luckless *Attis* who, similarly maddened by the Phrygian goddess Cybele, castrated himself under a pinetree. All in all, a nice derangement of epitaphs.

Pan Asleep

He half unearthed the Titans with his voice;
The stars are leaves before his windy riot;
The spheres a little shake: but, see, of choice
How closely he wraps up in hazel quiet!
And while he sleeps the bees are numbering
The fox-glove flowers from base to sealèd tip,
Till fond they doze upon his slumbering,
And smear with honey his wide, smiling lip.
He shall not be disturbed: it is the hour
That to his deepest solitude belongs;
The unfrighted reed opens to noontide flower,
And poets hear him sing their lyric songs,
While the Arcadian hunter, baffled, hot,
Scourges his statue in the ivy-grot.

T0964   One of Michael's finest english sonnets, written 15 January 1901 (ZJP
14b,OWF 1b)—possibly as a picture of Ricketts. When it was published in
WILD HONEY in the place of honour as the first poem (WDH 1), he
certainly took it to be so (OCQ 149o) and 'adored' it (ZJY 8a). For a while the poem
was considered as an *envoi* for the Pan and Syrinx masque SILENCE AND MUSIC
(OWB 27b), but it was dropped from the last surviving typescript OWC. That April
Ricketts completed a miniature portrait of Henry 'the face as if seen under a flash of
lightning' (ZJP 68a), then Shannon also came to draw her (OCK 117o *ICT: probably
the chalk study on back cover*). Michael, as ever, was undervalued and overlooked.

Pan Asleep: Pan is the Arcadian god of flocks, who also enjoys riot and noise. But
he prefers wild and lonely places, and you disturb him from his
noontide sleep at your peril.

Titans: The children of Uranus and Gaea. They were overcome by their
descendants Zeus and his brother gods, and put to flight, terrified by a
sudden great shout of Pan. Pan is renowned for the loudness of his
voice, which can drive men mad with fear ('panic').

reed: Pan once chased the nymph Syrinx from Mount Lycaeum to the River
Ladon, but there she hid and changed into a reed. It was from these
reeds he fashioned the shepherd's 'Pipes of Pan', still called a *Syrinx*.

Scourges: With squill. This was done if the flocks declined or game was scarce,
to encourage fertility; though it is hard to see how battery with
bluebells can have made any material difference. Squill acts as a
purge and emetic, and so was also used to ward off evil (probably with
equal success).

The Poet

Within his eyes are hung lamps of the sanctuary:
A wind, from whence none knows, can set in sway
And spill their light by fits; but yet their ray .
Returns, deep-boled, to its obscurity.

The world as from a dullard turns annoyed
To stir the days with show or deeds or voices;
But if one spies him justly one rejoices,
With silence that the careful lips avoid.

He is a plan, a work of some strange passion
Life has conceived apart from Time's harsh drill,
A thing it hides and cherishes to fashion

At odd bright moments to its secret will:
Holy and foolish, ever set apart,
He waits the leisure of his god's free heart.

T0986 A *sonnet libre* known from two undated autographs (H OWD 104b,M OWI
1b), and perhaps more probably Michael's work. Mary Sturgeon, the first
biographer, assumed that it was written in the 1880s and that it described
Henry (FMS 23-4); without access to the Journal or letters it would be impossible to
decide even if 'The Poet' was anything more than an abstraction, so she may be
forgiven for being wildly wrong on both counts. Actually, it is a picture of Thomas
Sturge Moore, whom they met for the first time in early June 1901: 'Moore, the Poet,
comes to dine with us... from illumined eyes gives worship to his god' (M ZJP 73b). It
is reasonable to assume that the piece was written shortly after; he even recognised
himself (ZCF 217or) when he read the published poem in WILD HONEY, WDH 58.
Moore later returned the compliment, with a poem (predictably) on Henry (VTM 26).
Michael, much earlier, had indeed written of Henry as a poet, or rather *dramatist*, in
T0221; and only the previous year (at the time of composition of DEIRDRE) in T0901.

The Poet:	Henry described him in a letter that September to her sister Amy, as "intensely modern, & in no wise decadent... a genuine new friend" (OCH 83a). So he was to remain (sa ZKD 86-7, MFC 60).
Within his eyes:	"In his eyes are hung the lamps of the sanctuary" (H ZJP 76a).
a dullard:	Moore's wife Marie took exception to this verse (YSH uf).
Time's harsh drill:	See again the first biography, FMS 243-4.
Holy and foolish:	Unmistakable traits of a monster (see T0947, note 2).

An Enchanter

To all men of the earth a foreigner,
He lends his alien glance to every eye;
The other side the moon he passes by,
And we too, of his freedom, double her.

We tingle with his rhapsody of sight,
And shiver in the coldness it employs;
Yet warmth the lizard from its slab enjoys
We feel the moment that we curse our plight.

From cunning distance his caress we take—
So wild things of the woodland please & mock:
In hours of gravity his thoughts forsake

His troubling mortals of the magic flock.
Ah, but his laugh detains us! He has need
His malice should enliven ears that heed.

T0988   This *sonnet libre* is known from two autographs, one in the hand of Henry
(OWD 105), the other in the hand of Michael (OWI 3b); neither is dated,
but the context of the second within other dated poems suggests the piece
was probably written some time in June 1901. It seems slightly more likely to have
been the work of Michael than of Henry. However the subject is not in doubt. It is a
vivid picture of Ricketts. There are other pictures of him in WILD HONEY including
the fancifully allusive T0964 and the more direct T0989; the latter was probably
written at the same time as T0988, and apart from internal evidence even has a
similar title, *Enchantment*. It is probably the very vividness, almost pungency, of the
picture of Ricketts in *An Enchanter* that precluded its publication at the time.

coldness: See also *The Ice-Country* (T1218) written in December 1905.
lizard: One of Michael's sharp, if affectionate, names for Ricketts— who was
to become aware of it (and be even more astonished to discover he
was also 'for years' known to Michael Field as "Fay" FCR 5). Much
later she wrote a *Green Lizard Sonnet*, so privately ambiguous that it
could be published without any fear of · decipherment by the
uninitiated (T1174); *Fay* is of course one aspect of the Enchanter.
wild things: A reference (through to verse 12) to Ricketts in his Pan *persona*,
developed more fully in T0964.

79

Eros of the Summits

Thou hast a land with air that sparkles, air
That pours crystalline round the blessèd heart
From mountain-holds, O Eros of the dart
Reversed, but not to figure death's despair—

Only that thou art cold of thy own power.
Where we too of thy power can mount to peace
Where all youth's torrent voices purl & cease,
Where Space is but to breathe, Time has no hour.

Under the shadow of thy wings we gaze
With steady light between them. All the ways
We take are 'mid thy plumes; & round our ears

In bands the snow white trumpet lilies blow
Wide over a beatitude of snow,
That never as the vale-snow disappears.

T0993   This unpublished poem recalls the first visit of the Berensons (married the
previous December) to Paragon 30 June 1901, the first time in fact they
had met since the rift of November 1895. The single autograph is
particularly interesting in being in Michael's hand, with revisions in the hand of
Henry (OWI 8b). Yet Henry is unequivocally the original author: 'In Eros of the
Summits I stammer the remembrance' (ZJP 90a sa ZKF 145r). She even goes on to
contrast the piece with the better known poem written by Michael on the identical
subject (*Chalices*, T0992): 'in *Chalices* Michael enters into my joy & peace, creating
them again... A gift indeed... from her hands'. *Chalices*, and to a lesser extent *Eros
of the Summits*, is unintelligible without recourse to the Journal account (ZJP 85-90).

land with air: Probably an indirect allusion to Italy, known to all four of them.
dart reversed: Induces friendship rather than passion. Henry had referred to this
                 once before in her song for Callirrhoë (T0198), with the obvious
                 new reference to her still volatile feelings for Berenson.
thou art cold: A curious, no doubt coincidental, echo from T0988.
trumpet lilies: Henry had gone to unusual pains for the visit: 'I stack my white
                 drawing-room at each end with lilies' (ZJP 85a). These lilies feature
                 prominently in Michael's poem; they are in fact the 'chalices'.

Elsewhere

Beauteous thou art, the spirit knows not how;
'Tis not the serpent-way thine iris slips,
Nor confluence of the temples and the brow,
Nor marge nor parting of the trembled lips:

Beauteous thou art; but never with thy face
Dwelleth thy beauty: all its riches are
Freighting for thee in distant argosies,
While thou art poor, save for a tranquil grace.

Beauty forever with the god doth keep
Backward, a few steps off, beside the shrine:
It is thy dreaming when thou art asleep;

Waking thou dost not wear it as a sign;
Yet wheresoe'er thou goest it limns thee, sweet,
As finest air a-quiver with the heat.

T0997   One of the handful of near-perfect sonnets that Michael wrote to Henry.
She was obviously fond of it, writing it out several times into her different
'fair copy' books; at least six autographs survive. The poem was written
19-20 July 1901 in *The Forest* (OWH 6b); they had left for Holmsley Cottage in the
New Forest (haunt of sawdust-challenged penguins, see T0936) on the 10th (ZJP
91b,ZCP 162). During the following five weeks they were to write much poetry. This
poem is in the form of a *sonnet libre*; there are varia in some of the autographs (as
YFB 11), but this is the final version printed in a magical sequence of such poems in
WILD HONEY (WDH 169) which make the author and the assignation inescapable
(WDH 165-181).

poor: It is worth a wilful misunderstanding of the text to record a Journal entry
three years later, where Michael remarks of some gift of Henry: 'He is
always finding some bit of money growing stale in his pocket, indeed
beginning to smell' (ZJS 163a). These ladies, heirs to a tobacco business,
and coal and iron ore mines, were not without means.

Visitants

Strange, on the lofty-builded boat,
The ferryman should weep!
Old Charon, avid still to note
The coin his crossings reap!
    Ruthless and plain to all,
With aspect like the foiling pall
Of his dire roof, our sweet sky's funeral.

Last night the dead, still more and more,
Had lowered his boat-side:
Those who beneath the mournful roar
Of a volcano died,
    In thousands, as they must,
Had each in turn his obol thrust
Into a palm that wearied of its lust.

Now on the shore no ghost— not one;
But with tired, stealthy eyes
The boatman saw a tumult run
Forward, as white dust flies.
    His palm itched, yet he bent
Reluctant on his oar, still spent
With waftage of those hosts to Hades sent.

On came the cloud, as if with feet
All plumes— a multitude
In clinging dance, their numbers fleet
To impetus subdued
    Of one fatality.
O Charon, what is this you see,
This snowy flock, a wind their Mercury?

They drift across the beamless slopes,
They drift upon the weeds
That do not dout them, streak the ropes,
Frost the giant river-reeds.
    They are but blossom-leaves,
O Charon, that a tempest cleaves
From orchards, or from hawthorn-hedge bereaves.

His oar drops down, his palms are pressed
Together at that sight:
His boat— the ferryman may rest,
And dream 'mid spectres white.
    He weeps their vanishing,
Who offer him no gold, but bring
The news that high on earth there has been spring

T1060   'I hear an exquisite poem of Henry's on the Spring's white blossoms drifted to hell'; so Michael in the Journal (ZJQ 83a). It is easy to agree— this has to be one of her most imaginative pieces. The poem was written 01 June 1902, as the draft autograph in Henry's hand verifies (OWQ 40-2), and eventually published in DEDICATED, DDD 90-1.

In the first week of May 1902 volcanic activity began in the Lesser Antilles, part of the Windward Islands group in the Caribbean. Throughout Wednesday 07 May 'horrible detonations' were heard as far away as Barbados, and the volcano *Soufrière* in the island of St. Vincent began to erupt, throwing up a column of smoke to 'a height of 8 miles'. There was darkness 'like midnight' and ashes and lava 2-4 feet in depth; 2000 people died. But worse was to come. On Martinique at 8 am the following day (Thursday 08 May) *Mount Pelée* tore apart with a tremendous explosion. The small town and port of St. Pierre was directly in the path of the 'rain of fire', lava and boiling mud. The subsequent pyroclastic flow when the plume collapsed was inescapable. *The Times* for May 14 reported 'A sailor named Prudent speaks of having seen men and women running hither and thither amidst the flames until a terrible cloud of smoke came, when they fell like flies' Some 30,000 people perished. These dreadful images were undoubtedly in Henry's mind when she wrote T1060.

Charon:	The ghosts of the dead must pay this miserly ferryman before he will take them in his boat across the River Styx.
dire roof:	Of Tartarus (the Underworld).
volcano:	Michael within a few days was to write *After Soufrière* (T1062), her own transformation of these events to mirror her bereft feelings when 'The Painters' left Richmond, coincidentally on 07 May.
obol:	Or obolus; a silver (later bronze) coin of ancient Greece, worth 1/6 of a drachma. Never gold (v41).
cloud:	A horrific allusion to the tumbling advance of volcanic ash.
Mercury:	Hermes in his role as *Psychopompos* (see note to T0281).
dout:	douse, i.e. extinguish as hot ashes.
blossom-leaves:	Suddenly and dramatically the image changes; here in Kensington at this time of year there are similar copious drifts of scurrying white petals in Abingdon Road, when the flowering cherries are wracked of their bloom. Nine years later Henry was to return to this trope in her preface to *The Orchard Floor* (selected passages from sermons by Vincent McNabb): 'the motion of wind as it plucks the orchards of blossom and makes for itself a plumage of paradise' (QOF v).

Silver movements, silver voices
  Women moving to & fro,
Where the garden-spices blow
  At the June day's summer-close.
  Daughter, mother,
Women gracious to each other—
  Now the plucking of a rose,
  Now the dropping of a hand
  Soft upon a flower-stand;
  Now a goddess stooping low,
  Now an angel glancing up,
  Now the raising of a head
  Lovely as the lifting up
  Of a flower from its cup,
    And beyond— a king is dead.
But that land is blest for ever,
  Safe, & healed, & happy so
Where sweet women pace together,
  Softly moving, speaking low.

T1064   The next-door neighbours at 2, The Paragon were Sir James and Lady
        Rivett-Carnac (ZJQ 83-4); they had a daughter Muriel (OKD 129). It was
        the voices of the two women drifting up from their garden which prompted
Michael to write this piece (ZJQ 99b sa OCJ 28,ZJY 73a). It was Midsummer Day
(24 June) 1902, two days before the planned Coronation of Edward VII (OWK 70b).

a king is dead: Edward had been reported 'indisposed' after attending a military
                tattoo at Aldershot on 14 June; the trouble was perityphlitis, and
                by late evening of 23 June his condition was causing concern. At
10 am on 24 June his medical advisers decided to operate; at about 12.30 pm Sir
Frederick Treves 'evacuated' a large abscess, though the royal appendix itself was
allowed to remain. The Coronation was postponed (in the event to August 9th); but
this very popular king did not die, so that Michael's gloomy prognostication was
somewhat premature. Both women enjoyed considerable holdings in *Thanatos Inc.*,
and Henry (in a favourite role of Pythoness) recorded in the Journal how she had
Foreseen It All: 'In the deep night... I woke with most omenous (sic) loading of the
Spirit (ZJQ 99b)... This catastrophe is the answer (ZJQ 100a)'.

The Woods are still

I

The woods are still that were so gay at primrose-springing,
Through the dry woods the brown field-fares are winging,
   And I alone of love, of love am singing.

II

I sing of love to the haggard palmer-worm,
Of love 'mid the crumpled oak-leaves that once were firm,
   Laughing, I sing of love at the summer's term.

III

— Of love, on a path where the snake's cast skin is lying,
Blue feathers on the floor, and no cuckoo flying;
   I sing to the echo of my own voice crying.

T1073   Known from three autographs, all in Michael's hand; it is probably her
work. Two have the partial date *Tue July 9* and the footnote *The Forest of
Wilverley enclosure* (OVY 37b,OWK 74b). The OWK text lies within a run
of dated 1902 pieces (ICT: in which July 9 was actually a Wednesday), but in July
1902 the Journal confirms they were staying at Wilverley Lodge (ZJQ 108b). The
OWK text bears the original title *Song. "I sing of love to the haggard palmer-worm"*,
as does the third autograph (OWD 109b). When published in WILD HONEY, WDH
22, it had no title; the one given here is that of the index. This was one of the first
poems to be popularised in anthologies in their life-times (AMS, AQC sa ZKC 138a).

field-fares: Large gregarious birds of the thrush (Turdidae) family, of birch and
               pine woodland. Often very noisy in flight, with a chacking, wheezing
               call. *T. pilaris* is a handsome bird with dove-grey head and rump,
               black tail, and a characteristic chestnut-brown tuxedo (faced on the
               breast with black arrowheads in a typical thrush pattern).
palmer-worm: A reference to Joel I 4: *That which the palmerworm hath left hath
               the locust eaten* (as also Amos IV 9). The actual palmer worm is a
               migratory hairy caterpillar with a voracious appetite, fittingly named
               for parasitic itinerant monks purporting to have come from the "holy"
               land (with a palm leaf to prove it). There may also be an allusion to
               Berenson here; back in 1894 they coined this new name for
               'Doctrine' because he had "eaten our years" (ZJG 132). When WDH
               was published in December 1907 there were references to the
               'haggard palmer-worm— that supreme cynic' in an exchange of
               letters with Amy (ZJX 59a, OCQ 1o).
blue feathers: Probably a jay, with memories of the previous August: see T1007.

85

Song. "She pulls one way her flowers"

I

The foxglove's flowers
Bend all one way
To the fair sea-south shining:
Of her inclining
She pulls one way her flowers

II

I love her leaning towers:
I love her that, uncheckt
As mortals pray
Amorous towards one aspect,
She pulls one way her flowers.

T1077   Wilverley Forest. Michael's hand, from prose by Henry: ' ...imperial with
fox-gloves. It is so beautiful that they are hung with bells only on one
side— it pulls them into leaning towers of such fine inclination' (ZJQ 112a).
Two autographs survive, both dated 13 July (*ICT: 1902*, OVY 40b, OWK 73b).

This is a typically delightful Michael Field flower lyric. *Digitalis purpurea*, with its tall,
unilateral racemes of pendulous bell-shaped flowers (usually pink, sometimes white),
is immediately recognisable. Foxgloves figured prominently in two much earlier
poems (T0552,602)

Pyramidal flashing forth crimson & white;

these were in the Luxembourg Gardens, at the time of the fraught Paris visits with
Berenson and Mary Costelloe, back in 1892 and 1893.

God's delight

I

There is white light around a wood,
And streaks of light that fall
It did not come in sudden blaze
As Jesus came to Paul,
But a white ray from whitest cloud
Singled me out among them all:
I only understood.

II

It is white light from God's delight,
It rests upon the road;
I do not ask why it should come
Nor what it may forbode,
Only for evermore there is
No briar upon my road
With God so clear in sight.

T1086   Michael recorded 'we drove to Boldre wood', probably the occasion of this
curious retelling of the Damascus road myth (Acts IX 3). Both autographs
(ZJQ 131a,OWK 88b) are in her hand, and dated August 03 (*ICT: 1902*).

A Dying Viper

The lethargy of evil in her eyes—
As blue snow is the substance of a mere
Where the dead waters of a glacier drear
Stand open and behold— a viper lies

Brooding upon her hatreds: dying thus
Wounded and broken, helpless with her fangs,
She dies of her sealed curse, yea, of her pangs
At God's first ban that made her infamous.

Yet, by that old curse frozen in her wreath,
She, like a star, hath central gravity
That draws and fascinates the soul to death;

While round her stare and terrible repose,
Vaults for its hour a glittering sapphire fly,
Mocking the charm of death.   O God, it knows!

T1090   Written by Henry 07 (?08) August 1902, towards the end of their Forest
holiday; she made a Journal entry 'In the morning I give our Dying Viper in
a "Sonnet Libre"' (ZJQ 135a). Another known draft exists (OWQ 45); the
piece was eventually published after her death in DEDICATED, DDD 93. Michael
Field wrote several memorable snake poems, including T0353, 996 and 1161.

A Dying Viper: The original title was The Dying Viper (ZJQ 132a). Vipera berus,
usually grey with a characteristic dark dorsal zigzag, prefers dry,
open country. Its venom is only rarely fatal to man.

lethargy of evil: They had spotted the adder a fortnight earlier. On 24 (?25) July,
Michael wrote in the Journal 'Yesterday we saw a dying viper...
there was a lethargy of evil in her eye' (ZJQ 127b sa 128-9).
There is also an echo of the 'implicating eyes' of La Gioconda
(T0453), the same

> patience in its rest
> Of cruelty that waits and doth not seek
> For prey

mere: A lake or pool.
God's first ban: Genesis III 14 sa T1486
sapphire fly: One of the Calliphoridae species.

Sweet-Basil

But thou art grown a symbol unto me!
Thy speech no more hath passion to entice;
As a sad, languorous wind thou art to me,
As a wind thwarted from the beds of spice.
To look upon thee in thy varying hour,
Thy moods, no more my spirit it contents;
Rhythm I feel of a remoter power,
And sway and falling of the elements.
Thou art no more thyself; I can no more
Reply to thee; thou art a boundless shore
That I am mute beside. Away, begone!—
Some potent semblance creep into thy stead,
Like that Sweet-Basil of the buried head,
A thing that I might brood and dote upon!

T1102   The previous May, Ricketts and Shannon had moved to 'The Palace'
(studios on the top floor of Lansdowne House in Lansdowne Road,
Holland Park W11), but the friendship of 'The Poets' and 'The Painters'
continued unabated. This poem was prompted by one of Ricketts's visits to
Richmond, and is almost certainly Michael's work; she completed it "Midnight" the
same day, 05 January 1903 (OWK 104b). In early drafts the title is unhyphenated,
and the quatorzain split 8/6. It was published in WILD HONEY, WDH 20.

Thy speech: 'Fay comes.... He has been having some new teeth in & still lisps
consciously' (H ZJR 6b).
shore: 'How like an estuary in soft mist he looks!' (H ZJR 6b).
buried head: An allusion to the DECAMERON of Giovanni Boccaccio, dating from
the Black Death of 1348; Filomena's tale (Fourth day, Novel 5).
Lisabetta's brothers kill her lover Lorenzo, who subsequently appears
to her in a dream. She finds his buried body, removes the head,
and puts it in a pot which she plants with roots of 'goodliest basil of
Salerno', watering it daily with her tears. The basil flourishes, her
brothers grow suspicious and remove the pot, discovering her secret.
She, bereft and still weeping, pines to death.

Camellias

To what deep fountains have they led desire?
From what deep-ambushed fountains have they drunk?
Sated in all their senses, they are sunk
Within themselves, nor languish, nor aspire.

Passion is in their substance, & the smell
The bosom smell of whiteness in their leaves—
All that, in secret, pearls & satins tell
Through yellow shadows of the breast that heaves.

And one of them— how lovely in her mode!—
One of them had the magic power to die;
Slid from the stem where she abode
With mournful violence: her petals lie,
Broke on the sudden from their mass, and all
The action stately as a funeral.

T1104   Those few who know Michael Field's work will instantly recognise the close
of this poem, which usually appears in isolation; it was published as such
(T1105) in WILD HONEY, WDH 80. Here for once is the original uncut
version. Dated 15 January 1903 (OWI 23b), it provides a further example of Michael
seizing on Henry's Journal descriptions (ZJR 9ab,11a), in this case of some camellias
they had bought. The following January they had shown the poem, with others, to
Ricketts, and he had found it 'even too long' (ZJS 18-22,OZL 152). It was
presumably at this time that the first two stanzas were finally discarded, after minor
adjustments had been tried; some of these tinkerings also survive (OWK 107b).

Logan Pearsall Smith admired the poem, though whether he saw the full
version is uncertain (ZKC 84). But it is curious he should relate the piece to Michael
Field having seen and 'celebrated that touching beauty' of Louise Kinsella. She was
indeed to be the subject of a later poem (T1131) but the tone of that was anything
but flattering. It was perhaps the *Traviata* undertones that led him to hypothesise
'Our poets saw her once in passing, and wrote the ...lines which show that they felt,
in her loveliness, the presage of her too-early death' (FLS 95).

The Lone Shepherd

I love but Love, yet must I change my god.
I leave the nestling of the wings sun-laced,
And hie to chaos where on earth's first sod
Eros is lonely shepherd of the waste.
There will be naught between us— not a prayer;
Nor has he any answer to my sighs;
Yet as I watch a music fills the air,
And one by one the stars break from the skies.
O Love, O Mystery, is it not thus—
Where the Madonna spreads her shining Child
We are not blest, there is no joy to us:
But we are broken, but we are renewed
Where, lone as that first Shepherd of the Wild,
The God spreads out His arms on Holy Rood.

T1128   Dated 15 August 1903, all the drafts are in Michael's hand, and the *incipit* uniquely tracks the essential drive if not ultimate outcome of her life (so FMS 64); the first title was *The lonely Shepherd* (OWK 125b).   On one autograph someone, possibly Ricketts, has written *fabulous* (OWD 5b); on another, a footnote reads *before Haslemere* (OVY 57b). Michael sent a copy of this poem, with others, to Ricketts the following January. He visited on the 25th, when Henry read the poems to him: 'Finally I read...<u>The Shepherd of the Wild</u>. He greatly praises the great exposition of the first line— a Master's way of beginning; but he objects to "O Love O Mystery". (ZJS 18a,22a). Michael as usual took this to heart; the OVY and OWD drafts are 'corrected', and it is this version that was eventually published in WILD HONEY, WDH 38. The present text is the original; one cannot help thinking the Poet was a better judge than the Painter.

O Love, O Mystery: Michael altered this to   *Thus it must be— is it not ever thus?*

91

A Symbol

Sweet, my abode is by the running brooks
Covered by leaves the water purls along;
I cannot watch its charm of silvery looks,
But from the hollow feel its muffled song.
Why, by that covert do I love to rest,
To hear in secret what I cannot see;
Is it, one sense being held in strict arrest
The other vaunteth of its liberty?
Love, it is this: for the dear symbol's sake
I love the darkened music of this den:
Since of thy absence my sad heart must break
Except thou give thyself to me again.
Will not a letter give me all my theme
As that low murmurous sluice reveals the stream?

T1129   This english sonnet is found in two manuscripts, both in Michael's hand and
dated 24 August 1903, with a footnote *the cottage, Fernhurst*. Untitled in
OVY 58ab, it appears to correspond to the alternative title *The Stream's
Secret* in the Index (OVY 64). The addressee is unquestionably Ricketts (sa v4 in the
variant sestet below), at that time on the continent; Michael had already written to
him in Dresden on the 22nd 'commanding' to be sent his photograph (ZJR 108a).

abode: Michael Field is guest for five weeks in Mary Berenson's cottage
                    Kingshott at Fernhurst (near Haslemere, Surrey) OWK 126b. Mary
                    had written 'You are the first inhabitants of my Cottage, &
                    probably you will be the dearest for all time' (ZJR 101a). The one
                    drawback is 'the small tyrant' (M ZJR 154b, see T1132).
thy absence: There is also a variant sestet (OVY 58a)

                        Love it is thus; for the dear symbol's sake
                        I love the darkened music of this den;
                        Sweet profit of the magic do thou take
                        And paint me all thy spirit with a pen,
                        For if from every sense thou bar the way
                        What have I but the grave of yesterday?

                    As Henry remarks in the Journal, 'I am not at all so sure God
                    loves Fay, but oh... Michael does' (ZJR 162b).

Demi-God

God of a yet chaotic hierarchy!
When the new realms are won, the sceptres crowned,
Mindful of Aphrodite, mild, profound,
With temples crystal as the crystal sea,

One will enthrone how gradual on the light,
Where air and light and thought have finer sense;
Then . . . but till then the mystery how tense,
Strain of the veil, and thwarting of the sight!

We cannot serve him; lone he perseveres.
Created ripe as Hermes, with a theme
That is himself, his faculties, his dream,

He strives for converse with us through the years:
And only as we break our jealous pains,
And listen with charmed spirit, he attains.

T1132 A Journal entry by Henry for Sunday 07 (ICT ?06) September 1903 reads:
'Michael writes all but the last couplet of a Sonnet libre on Bernhard', so we
may be surprised, but fairly confident, who the Demi-God is; the final
couplet follows on the facing page (ZJR 138ab). The withering directness of Michael's
following poem T1133, as also Henry's later pronouncement "all-judging little Jove"
(ZJR 152a) make the matter certain. And yet the sense remains ambiguous. Henry
wrote 'Beauty is that which lies at the very bottom of vitality' (ZJR 120a), and it is this
Beauty which does also seem to be directly addressed. There are at least three other
extant autographs, one with the sonnet split 4,4,4,2 (ORR 2); the version printed here
is that published in WILD HONEY, WDH 59. The matter, as well as the manner,
recalls Baudelaire's *La Beauté*, which Michael(?) translated two years before (T1020).

serve him: Berenson or Beauty? Perhaps Michael maliciously imples a little
                    of each; this allows the sestet two wildly divergent readings, and
                    an astonishing sourness.
ripe as Hermes: According to legend, a precocious child who stole a herd of
                    Apollo's cows, AND invented the lyre, using some of the cow-gut
                    and the shell of a tortoise, while still in swaddling bands.
dream: One of Berenson's *dicta*, "Art is symbolic. It is a Dream" (ZJR
                    120a). And again, "Essential poetry, where the Dream fills
                    language with itself, is very rare" (ZJR 134a). One cannot fault
                    'the Doctrine' in this.   sa T0977

Onycha

I would be dumb to thee, I would be dumb,
Not as a star that has a tale to tell,
Not as a flower that whispers what befell,
— Shut solitary with her spice and gum,
When she was flower, & heard the wild bee's hum:
As a white, pure white, silver-sealèd shell
To slip down to thy heart's floor, & there dwell
Secret to thee for ever, I would come.

There would be no expectance in my state,
No memories would be with us, & no sound,
And I might be forgotten— I should be
Washed o'er again as by Infinity,
Remote upon a seldom-trodden ground,
And of thy busy brain left desolate.

T1147   There are two poems with this title, the more well-known (T0952) printed in
WILD HONEY, WDH 14. Both are undoubtedly Michael's work, and though
the dedicatee of the first is undoubtedly Henry (who for a while becomes
'Onycha' ZJO 179-80), it is at least possible the second is addressed to Ricketts. The
two poems have a common theme and central image (the shell), but this alternative
version (OWD 23b) has never before been published. Two of the three extant
autographs are dated 22 December 1903; OWK 132b has a footnote *The gold
room*. Onycha II (as it is distinguished in the Journal) was one of the poems sent to
Ricketts for his approval the following January (ZJS 18,22). Michael knew the value
of what she had achieved; in a letter to her younger niece Amy Ryan she says "I
wrote last night one of the divinest sonnets Heaven has ever given me" (OCK 102o).

Onycha: Aromatic *nail*-like operculum of the wing-shell (*Strombus,* a tropical
ocean conch and cousin of the whelk), used in incense in Mosaic ritual.
dumb: The early draft (OVY 64a) offers a variant incipit:

To thee for evermore I would be dumb

shell: Shells were in favour at Paragon that Christmas and bought for
presents from 'Sowerby Shells' at Kew (ZJR 209b). Henry wrote in the
Journal 'Shells are like buried Air— air made a treasure' (ZJR 215a).
sa T1151-2

To the Lord Love

I am thy fugitive, thy votary,
Nor even thy mother tempts me from thy shrine:
Mirror nor gold, nor ornament of mine
Appease her: thou art all my gods to me,
And I so breathless in my loyalty
Youth hath slipped by and left no footprint sign:
Yet there are footsteps nigh. My years decline.
Decline thy years? Burns thy torch duskily?
Lord Love, to thy great altar I retire;
Time doth pursue me, age is on my brow,
And there are cries and shadows of the night.
Transform me, for I cannot quit thee now:
Love, thou hast weapons visionary, bright—
Keep me perpetual in grace and fire!

T1155 An italian sonnet with a chequered history, recast from several variant drafts of *A Petition* (T1139), written by Michael the previous November. Ricketts was in her mind then: *Who prate of friendship reaching to the night,/ While Passion of itself doth hotly fire—* (OWK 129b). It seems it was a fresh event that caused her to reconsider the old sonnet and produce the new one, less personal, less direct, but no less with Ricketts as its focus. She started a new exercise book and *To the Lord Love* was the first entry, dated 27 January 1904 (OWJ 1b). There were two footnotes, one domestic: *they are distempering the sun-room* ; and one which details the event that probably triggered the rewrite: *Fay brought the star-sapphire ring on Monday.* This was the gift he had promised her, a truly extraordinary ring that Shannon named 'Solomon'. She may have read too much into this, and perhaps who can blame her? (sa OZM 101). It seems to have been Sturge Moore who added the epigraph *At the approach of old age* (SMF 42). That December she was to write in the Journal 'This spring age fell upon me' (ZJS 204a). Whatever its background, this is a wonderful poem. It was originally published in WILD HONEY, WDH 37.

Lord Love:	Eros
thy fugitive:	One autograph has a (deleted) variant : *I am thy pilgrim & thy votary* (OVY 61a)
thy mother:	Aphrodite is implied; his father was possibly Hermes, but the parentage of Eros is controversial.
years decline:	Michael was then 57, and Ricketts 37.
torch:	Used to set hearts on fire.
great altar:	At Thespiae, where Eros was worshipped by the Boeotians as a phallic pillar.

The moonlight lies a pavement on the grass,
The forest is dark air against the sky—
I leave my chow-dog by the fire, and pass
The window-pane on to the void. A cry
Behind me, on my track, sharp as the sight
Of injured ghost, intrepid in its pain,
And whimsical as effort of a sprite
To do an errand on the earth again!
A cry— my knowledge of the heart it wrings
Has held me many years from liberty,
From Anet, and from Blois; and, as I live,
The motion of that tender vocative
Shall stay my foot from all those dreamèd things,
And all the diverse kingdoms over sea.

T1169   On 13 July they took a seven week Forest holiday (ZJS 107-30), and in late
August Michael recorded in the Journal 'Last night we leant against the
little forest-gate— to see the black forest in its mass, & the moon. (Whym
Chow).. left shut up in the parlour— lifted foxlike cries... that... will prevail over Anet,
& Diane' (ZJS 135-6). The sonnet has a footnote *The Forest, finished at home Aug
29, 1904* (ZJS 138a). There are two other autographs (OWK 145b,OYR 5) but
neither these nor the published text (WILD HONEY, WDH 187) bear a title. When
Sturge Moore published it (SMF 74), he added the eminently exact *Continental trips
forgone for the sake of Whym Chow.* This dog would keep them in Britain six more
years (ZKA 123a); in 1901 they had had 'to give up Scotland' when it was ill (ZJP
123a sa OCJ 183r). An exasperated Mary Berenson in 1905 compared their
durance to that of Oscar Wilde: "Chow... immobilizes you as much as if you were in
Reading Gaol" (ZCE 208r). Michael sent a copy of the sonnet to Ricketts 'that you
may learn what vows & what devotion nice behaviour stir in Michael' (OWD 28); and
it was probably another that went in the dog's coffin in January 1906 (ZJV 23a).

lies: The verb is of course intransitive, but needs a following comma.
Anet: Their chief preoccupation in summer 1904 had been *Dian(e),* 'our new
            play' (ZJS 116). Diane de Poitiers, (1499-1566), duchesse de Valentinois
            and mistress of Henri II, Queen of France in all but name, inevitably
            fascinated. *Anet* was the site of her splendid Renaissance château, to
            which she was 'retired' by the rightful Queen, Catherine de Médicis,
            after Henri's death in 1559. *Blois* was almost the second capital in this
            period; here Catherine died in 1588, in her 'room with secret panels'.

Green Lizard Sonnet

O Love, the transformations thou hast given!
Love, through all transformations I believe.
The Jove that I have seen casting his levin
I wear as a green lizard on my sleeve. . .
Love, Love! Can'st thou take on such utter dearth,
Nor lovely as the moon in lapse of powers,
Nor burning frangipanni at the hearth,
Nor with soft incense incensing the hours?
Why move so alien, why art thou thus?
Wear any mask, so thine eyes pierce the shaft,
Or turn thee wailing to thy Genius:
Sighs are there that to me thou can'st not waft,
Imaginations, hopes that must divide—
Yet, as thou art a god, interpret wide!

T1174   There are two autographs, both in Michael's hand and dated 8-10 November 1904 (OWJ 8b,OWK 147b). Both are also titled *The* Green Lizard Sonnet. This, one of Michael's many sonnets, is one of the few actually to *have* the word 'sonnet' in its title; it is particularly ironic therefore that the published version in WILD HONEY (WDH 19) is a bewildering triskaidekain, having mislaid its verse 9 (presumably through a printer's oversight). Here, it is restored from the autographs, and the poem is once more a respectable english sonnet. Ricketts is the theme; recently he had not been sufficiently attentive. In a Journal entry for 18 November, Michael wrote 'I tell Painter I have written a furious sonnet against him called the <u>Green Lizard Sonnet</u>' (ZJS 181a).

levin: Lightning; this is Jove in his role as Fulgurator, the Sky God. His *transformations* for amorous dalliance are numerous, as T0511.

lizard: This was one of their names for Ricketts; Michael had 'bought a lizard' at the end of 1903 (presumably not a live one, ZJR 196b), and Ricketts appears as 'Eve's pretty lizard' in a limerick possibly by Henry (T1186).

frangipanni: Amy had sent a box of frangipanni (perhaps the red jasmine, P. rubra) for 'the great Birthday' (ZJS 163b: Michael was 58 on 27th October). On 08 November they were burning it (ZJS 176b ?the dead flowers); the Journal has several references to scent-sniffing around this time.

Genius: A guardian spirit similar to the Greek *dæmon*, which according to the Romans came into existence with the man to whose life it was bound.

A Japanese Print

Love, I have found a symbol of our state,
What to ourselves we are: of this no hint
As we twain walk together, nor give glint
Of happy knowledge, or of eyes' debate.
Behold the pearl embedded in our fate,
And treasure of our secret in this print
Of women meeting: face & action stint
The vibrant joy; nor has one come too late
And earned reproach; nor is there any word
Or flutter of the breast, or garment stirred. -
Only one stoops with humbler strain to reach
The greeting arms bent down to her, & each
Small hand becomes a ceinture, as the hasp
Of a fair bracelet fastens on its clasp.

T1178   There are two autographs of this italian sonnet, both in Michael's hand and
dated Thursday 24 November 1904 (YFB 17). Michael (for it must be she)
changed her mind several times over the title. The Journal autograph has
Fellowship scored through, then *Of Meeting*; then her third and presumably final
choice, the precise title given here (ZJS 181b). However the YFB draft reverted to
Fellows, and the fellowship of Michael Field is certainly the subject. *Fellows* may
have been dropped since it had already been used twice by Henry for poems on
classical subjects (T1008,89); *Fellowship* was to be the title of one of the last ever
Michael Field poems, the very moving T1721, written after Henry's death by the
dying Michael in the Spring of 1914.

symbol: There were, in their lives together, at least two others (OYS 19o,ZKA 229a).
pearl: This was to be a third (T1269):in a poem perhaps by Henry (ZKC 89).
print: Michael discovered this on a visit to the 'Palace' when both Painters were
out (ZJS 180b); it probably belonged to Shannon, who had an interest in
Japanese art. Some 23 years previously William Schwenck Gilbert had
siphoned the renal flow of the Aesthetic Movement when he had
Bunthorne, his 'fleshly' poet, roundly declare:

> I do *not* care for dirty greens/ By any means.
> I do *not* long for all one sees/ That's Japanese.

However, the chrysanthemum culture was to reach another peak with the
White City Exhibition of 1910.
ceinture: girdle

O to be in Lulworth
Now that Puss is there!
and who ever wakes in Lulworth
Feels, with sudden blank despair,
That the whippets below will come to grief,
And to kill a Cat wd give much relief,
For the Skin-Flint grudges the hen & sow,
    In Lulworth now

And after Easter the space that follows
When the inside groans from its awful hollows
See, where her precious Spouse to the dull edge
Of appetite shows how they live in clover—
Sardines & biscuits! At the wide tin's edge
That's his last fish. . . She boils each egg twice over,
Lest you should think she never cd recapture
Her first fine country rapture.
But tho the prospect looks a little blue,
All will be well when Daisy's milked anew
For bowls of milk, the little children's dower,
Far Wholesomer than flesh or pastry-flour

T1198   This exists as an isolated autograph in Henry's hand at the back of the
         Journal for 1905 (ZJT 159a), and is probably her work. Dating it more
         precisely is not easy; Easter (if v9 is a serious indicator) in 1905 fell on the
weekend 21-3 April. The work is readily recognisable as a parody of Browning's
Home-thoughts, from abroad; Michael (perhaps) had taken liberties with this poem
once before (T0585). Henry's version involves a familiar butt of the variety stage, the
seaside landlady— one with whom they stayed in July 1903; this experience had
prompted Michael to burst into French, *J'ai faim à mourir* (T1125). sa OCK 9o

Puss: A family name for Amy. When the Ryans had their seaside break is not
         clear; it *might* have been around Easter. By July 7 Edith recorded 'The
         brother & sister come to say goodbye before Ireland' (ZJT 81b).
grief: Perhaps the whippets (and the Cat?) may be candidates for the menu.
         Henry has scrawled this phrase, which might also be read *cause/ O grief*.
         This alternative seems to make little sense.

The Mask

How bold the country where we danced . . .
Great uplands, headed dark
With trees, as if night's sombre mark
Had sealed the vivid pasture hers,
With seal of convocated firs—
A noble country by her sign enhanced.

How wide the air and silence too,
A single bird's wing heard,
Save for the voices 'neath the bird
Of masqueraders on bright grass.
"Whose is this form I cannot pass?
Who is she?" And they breathed a name I knew.

She passed me in black velvet mask,
Black as the fir-knolls, black
As they upon the fields. Alack!
Why must I see her as once seen,
With tender pearl of face, a sheen
Of childhood in her face? What would I ask?

She came as comes a wind that treads
Round hill-brows in the night;
We stood together: "Oh, for sight
Of thee, my lost for many years!
I have forgotten, in my fears,
The way the hair about thy forehead spreads."

Powerless the Masker stood: I laid
The velvet softness by.
The curving mask . . . Oh, I should die
To speak the bare face underneath;
It were the last moan of my death . . .
In cottage-smoke of age it will not fade.

I shrieked and fled— how slow my feet,
And wild as they were chained!
She fled . . . but where she stood remained
The empty sable mask. Alas,
That I had cast it on the grass—
O silent pastures and the bird's wing-beat!

T1205   From a Journal entry we know that Henry was at work on this mysterious
and evocative poem 07 August 1905: 'During the long morning I write the
Velvet Mask' (ZJT 97a). They had been revisiting their old home in
Derbyshire, a re-awakening of unhappy memories for Henry. 'One must never meet
the Past face to face in its nakedness— one must leave the black velvet mask on that
face, or all is marred' (ZJT 92b sa ZJH 158b). The reason emerges in a later entry: 'I
have borne— again the pains & inflictions of childhood' (ZJT 104a). There is a single
surviving autograph (OWQ 63); the poem was published after her death in
DEDICATED, DDD 107-8.

convocated: Called together (by the night); a striking image, recalling T0321's
sacred wood.

noble country: They had arrived at Dovedale on 19 July, stopping over at the *Izaak
Walton*; they then moved on to Ashbourne, Newton and Ilam. By
the 27th they were at Hanson Grange, Tissington, and on the 29th
in Alsop. They remained in the neighbourhood some further ten
days, and revisited Newton Leys, Parwich, where the family had
lived 1867-73.

Who is she?   If someone more real than an abstract Past, an actual woman, there
are two apparent possibilities: her dead mother ('lost for many
years'), or her sister ('childhood in her face'), first married, and now
living in Ireland. But surely if anyone actual is implied, it could only
be Henry herself. It is only from a meeting with the *doppel-gänger*
that she would have 'shrieked and fled'.

101

Christening gifts

Stir the embers that his eyes
Wonder at the sparkling cries
And the glitter of the fire.
Pile the coals a little higher
That the crackling flame be sped
In a glory round his head!
And— well-ordered & intent
To my gifts the babe consent.

First a feather from the wing
Of an angel, shadowing,
Then, profuse in dew that wets,
Stuff his fists with violets;
And, beside these, do not miss
Yellow leaves of strawberries
That the wild fruits may be his
Though November should forbid:-
Sea-wrack mid the plants be hid
Bubbling brine, that he may be
Certain lover of the sea:
And of common stones some store
That the little one may know,
As the wisest long ago,
Ocean's hollows to explore
Picking pebbles on the shore.

T1212   Thomas Sturge Moore's son Daniel Charles Sturge Moore was born 05
November 1905, "dear little Guy Faux, for he was born on that day" (OZL
224 sa ZCF 208o). Michael, then with Henry at Court House, Rottingdean,
recorded in the Journal 'I am chiming some small verses to his babyhood' (09
November, ZJT 121a). A single draft of *Christening Gifts*, undated, has luckily
survived (OCZ 31), and with it a sachet containing feathers and sea-wrack. Young
Dan was to receive more expensive christening gifts (OCK 179-80) but surely none
as magical and memorable; sa OCZ 23-6 and T1213.

embers :   Not necessarily a reference to his date of birth! Michael wrote to Thomas
and Marie from Court House: 'And make a fire of coals on the hearth—
.. I would stretch him as Demetia stretched her nursling in the flame—
that he may really see the living spirits in the embers' (OCZ 24o).
shore :   Possibly an allusion to Newton's famous humble self-description.

Requiescat

I call along the Halls of Suffering!
Hark! Down each aisle reverberated cries
Out of deep wounds, out of each fiery spring
Of nerve, or piteous anguish of surprise.

And I must traverse these grand vaults to hear
The patter of thy feet, my little Chow,
Driven soft of frenzy on and on— the drear
And winter bee-note at thy stricken brow.

Loud Halls, O Hades of the living! On! . . .
What, are the swarming little cries not heard?
What, are the lit bright feet for ever gone
Or yet to swifter orbit they were spurred?

If I should wander on till Time had close
Thee, with thy shuffled paws, I should not find:
No chasm, nor any heinous shadow knows
Thy haunt; nor may I fear thee left behind.

Forth, Forth! Away! He is not of these Halls—
No motion of him there, Whym Chow no sound:
His ruby head shall never strike their walls,
And nowhere by a cry shall he be found.

T1222   No autograph is known, but the poem was published twice, in WILD
HONEY (1908), and WHYM CHOW Flame of Love (1914); the text printed
here is that of the final version, WCF 9. The earlier version WDH 188-9
has the alternative title *Halls of Suffering*, and differs slightly in matters of
punctuation as well as a significant word difference in v12. Sturge Moore included
the piece in SMF but cut it savagely. It is almost certainly part of the set written by
Henry in early 1906: 'my Chow-Poems welled' H ZJV 27a.

Requiescat: *May he rest* ; Chow's death presaged the last of the halcyon days.
And I must::   This, and the following stanza, is omitted in SMF.
spurred: WDH reads *stirred*. In mid-January 1906 the dog developed a form of
meningitis, and 'whirled round like a stately were-wolf with such
terrible rhythm as drew the imagination into its circles' (H ZJV 16a).
shuffled: SMF has *muffled,* but Moore may have used a variant manuscript.

Better to think of thee as underground
     In peace profound,
The purple hellebore about thy head
     Where the brow bled
And rest, long waves of rest breaking across thy brain.
     O little Chow, my Sweet,
Thou with stayed feet to watch for me again?
Nay, I will sue for peace— thou canst not bear the strain,
Watching from out Eternity's lone house
     As from a window-pane.
Nay— I would yield thee to the roses gone,
  The sweet thoughts, thought upon,
  The blinking years, rather than so
     Keep up thy woe.
But I will pray the living things
Seated about the throne with wings,
To loose thee to my footprints track.
Thou shalt divine, though I may lack.
Yea, thou shalt hear my Voice, though till Death come
  I of the yearnling cries am dumb.
     I will go lone, so Heaven provide,
Secure, thou trottest at my side,
With me at my uprising— by my bed,
Even as God with David tho' he fled—
My prayer for thee; for in this wise,
Only by being where thy Sahib lies
Art thou, O little Chow, in Paradise.

T1253   A single untitled Journal autograph in Michael's hand, dated 26
        February 1906 (ZJV 43b). The essence of the poem is v18; Michael
wrote to Amy later that Henry's poems on the dog's death 'break
one's heart' (OCM 78r), but they can seem laboured and art-ful when compared
with the simple directness and clear-eyed love of her own. This poem seems to stem
from Henry's reading of *Absence*, T1242 (ZJV 40a).

hellebore: The Christmas rose *H. niger*, which would be in flower in January.
brow bled: Whym Chow, the brave little soldier, received his *quietus* on the 28th
          January with a bullet through the brain (ZJV 18b,22-3).

To find thee I could wander through the world
Through its huge forests, tangled in the night,
Over Sahara with its sands up-swirled
As manes of angry lions— over the white,
And uncrushed snowfields or the plains of grass.
I crave a universe round which to pass
In search of thee, to traverse stream & height
'Neath clouds of darkness, under breadths of light

Oh, but the ache! For thee to pine & be
Myself even as an animal forlorn,
Seeking in restless pain to follow thee,
As thou hadst sought had thy beloved been torn
From thee! For hours I leave my humankind,
And rove a'drift; yea, seem to snuff the wind—
On, on, in wonder that such love was born
As drives me on only to seek & mourn.

blinking:　　Passing in the twinkling of an eye.
living things:　The Seraphim, of the alarming visions of Ezekiel I 5-6 and Isaiah VI 2.
　　　　　The 'fiery flying serpents' may have been electrical storms, but they are
　　　　　traditionally described as ecstatically adoring, and said to 'burn with
　　　　　love' (*sāraph* to burn), so are eminently appropriate to this occasion.
divine:　　Be made aware.
David:　　Opportunist second king of Israel c 1000 BC (I Samuel 16 / I Kings 2).
Sahib:　　Victoria had become Empress of India in 1876, and the British *Raj*
　　　　　seemed likely to last for ever; *sāhib*— an Urdū word from the Arabic
　　　　　for *friend*— became the respectful manner of address used by native
　　　　　Indians towards virtually any European male.

T1263　　A Journal draft dated 23 April 1906 is in Michael's hand (ZJV 81b);
　　　　　one other autograph exists, undated, in Henry's (OWO 103o). Neither
　　　　　is titled. It is difficult to decide who is the primary author, but since the
poem seems based on prose by Henry (ZJV 78a), and bearing in mind Michael's
predilection to 'cast into poetry', the balance seems marginally in her favour. Also, if
the piece is Henry's, why was not this fine lyric published with the majority of other
chow poems, indisputably by Henry, in WHYM CHOW, FLAME OF LOVE ? Whatever
the solution, it seems likely that Henry had a part in it.

the ache:　　'an ache not to be put by. O Chow, the ache!' H ZJV 78a

Whym Chow

Nay, thou art my eternal attribute:
Not as Saint Agnes in loose arms her lamb,—
The very essence of the thing I am:
And, as the lion, at Saint Jerome's suit,
Stood ever at his right hand, scanning mute
The hollows of the fountainous earth, whence swam,
Emerging from the welter, sire and dam:
While Jerome with no knowledge of the brute
Beside him, wrote of later times, of curse,
Bloodshed and bitter exile, verse on verse
Murmuring above the manuscript (in awe
The lion watched his lord, the Vulgate grew),
So it was wont to be betwixt us two—
How still thou lay'st deep-nosing on thy paw!

T1264   Written by Michael 13 May 1906 (ZJV 88b, sa 26b); the Oxford
         autograph has a footnote May— *tulip-bud-Sunday* (OWK 166b). When
         the poem was eventually published in WILD HONEY (WDH 191) in 1908,
the Ryans had been living in their final home Grove House in Milltown, Dublin some
two years. Michael wrote to Amy: 'There can be no picture of me— nor must I ever
be thought of— without Whym. That is what I try to say in the Sonnet' (OCS 16o, sa
OCM 78r). The photograph taken perhaps in 1903 (YCA 3,ZJV 47b), and
reproduced on the front cover of this book, must have gratified her; the Radio 3
broadcast of the poem by the BBC in June 1980, in Roy Fuller's tribute to Michael
Field, would surely have pleased her even more.

Agnes: Obstinate girl beheaded c 304 in Rome by Diocletian, possibly an
            overreaction to malapertness. Usually represented with a lamb as symbol
            of purity, perhaps through the further slippery allusion *agnes/agnus*.
Jerome: Eremitical self-mortifier aka Hieronymus, aka Sophronius, c 347-420. In
            Rome, as a secretary to Pope Damasus, he was commissioned with
            translation of the old and new testaments into Latin 383-405.
welter: An allusion to Genesis VIII; v9-10 apply to the remainder of the OT.
in awe: Sturge Moore renders the parenthesis in italic (SMF 74).
lion: Associated with Jerome presumably as founder of Latin monasticism, or
            perhaps as a symbol of strength. One is reminded of Aulus Gellius's tale
            of Androclus, the runaway Roman slave who extracted a thorn from the
            very sore paw of a similar beast; and the further elaboration of his
            subsequent fatal encounter in the arena. Different lion, boom-boom.
Vulgate: Latin bible, literally the 'common' version, as translated by Jerome.

Bowed to the waters by their heavy treasures,
  Behold these ships fraughted with prayers,
Not with strange marvels— with the very pleasures
    For which we pant:
Beneath these towered masts the things we want.

Looming the vessels & antique of fashion,
Through noble clouds slowly the trireme bears:
It is the suppliant, slave's cry of passion
    That, in their pride,
Draws these huge galiots to the water-side.

T1271   There are undated drafts of this piece in an Oxford manuscript (OWK
168a,327o), and a Journal autograph dated 03 July 1906 (ZJV 118b). All
are untitled, in Michael's hand, and probably her own work. In another
four years she was to write two more memorable poems on the theme of prayers,
as letters to God; which surely they are (T1574-5). But the wonderful trope of T1271
seems to have been derived from the spectacle of the slow-moving Thames barges
passing Paragon, especially at night. These were a constant presence and continuous
source of potent imagery:

> *As in the night I watch the genius*
> *Of the great barges flicker on the wall:*
> (*Reality* T1051, sa T0893,925)

In early July she had written in the Journal: 'We are tortured of worry & care— but
slowly as ships of heavy treasure our prayers come in...' (ZJV 111a).

fraughted: laden
trireme: An ancient Greek, and later Roman, galley with three ranks of oars; often
        these were used as ships of war.
galiot: Another ancient Roman galley; but also applied to Dutch cargo-boats.

In Aznac

"They murdered him, my father's son, beloved,
And all the flood of life in me is moved.
Weltering, furrowed, the enormous flood,
And full of means to fructify— the mud
Of Nile is in the motions of my pulse;
Sources from mystic, ancient hills convulse
My powers, distracting, while their purpose grows,
And inundation from their centre flows.
Even in their shallows, where their dalliance smiles,
The things they play with are jagged crocodiles. . . .
And there are lotuses, with sceptred stems,
And cushioned on their leaves their diadems.
Compelled to wax and welter through my soul,
The dark and spiral tides diffusive roll:
They shall be poured out from their patience soon;
For hours ago To-day passed by its noon."

    And all the afternoon
Had Queen Nitocris smoothed the myrtle oil
    Round her fair cheeks of roses famed.
    And all the afternoon
She had wound Egypt's double serpent's coil
    Till doubling on her brow it flamed.
    And all the afternoon
She had been choosing necklaces and chose
    One of winged scarabs rare.
    And all the afternoon
She watched upon her emerald dress the glose
    Of moonstone lotuses embroidered there.
    And all the afternoon
She spoke impassively to vassals black,
    And the chief Eunuch came and went:
    For all the afternoon,
High to her mirror or when falling back,
    She planned some craft of merriment.

How the sun set in blaze of red,
The rapine of its flambeaux spread
Across the land, across the stream! . . .
Night ruled as though no day had been.

The palace by the water cast
Gleams upward from its bases vast,
As from a dancer's feet shoot out
Bright rays that in ascension flout
The radiance from the neck and face:
Athwart the river-current's race
So glows the palace from below
With festival, as fishers know
Who seek their catch upon the Nile.
"The great Room will be used" they smile;
"And we should be down there to see
And join the pampered revelry."

In the deep hall below the stream
Torchlit the golden vessels gleam,
And ruby bowls of lucid glass;
And flowers there are in sating mass,
As a whole land were stripped of flowers.
While fruit is offered under bowers
Of urgent blossoms that would draw
Want out of surfeit: on the floor
Perfumes no man should breathe— but die,
And breathe of them immortally.

Surely, the bidden guests are prized!
For Queen Nitocris, tranquillized
From all her woe, is with the troop.
See, how she rises; see, how stoop
The double snake-heads in her hair,
And how she smiles to be so fair,
And bid such eager eyes adieu—
But it is meet that she withdrew
And gave the feasters unzoned mirth.
She rises, as a goddess leaves the earth;
And surging in her loveliness of pride,
Her panoply— as peacock-feathers glide,
Eyeing observers of the peacock's show—
Surges, and follows round her, to and fro,

And sweeps, exultantly aware, the gaze,
With lengths of emerald tissue and its glaze
Of moonlight and its blues of hollow night:
While all her scarabs clatter, like a flight
Of night-birds. And the Queen, the Fair One, gone,
'Mid shouts, there is none else to look upon.

"The night is hot for feasters in my vaults,
        Now that excess no longer halts,
                Now it is free;
And shouts come up from far beneath the stream,
        No more acclaiming, it would seem,
                My power nor me.
Lo, is there change, a gurgle of the tide?
        My palace drinks, beatified,
                The waters black,
Bitter as sea-slime, of the weedy Nile.
Drink, Aznac, drink, my House, beguile
                Your thirst nor lack;
Engorge the volume of your lust, fill deep
        The entrails of your building steep!
                I see no more
The dazzle in the waters from your feast;
        The torches' mounting rays have ceased,
                Dead to the core;
The seaweeds and the river weeds now rush
        Unlit along, in tangles lush;
                Yet are there cries,
Not sprung of wine; O Nilus, of thy draught,
        That by the feasters must be quaffed,
                As each one dies,
Who killed my brother Papi, in the swirl
        Of upper waters as they hurl
                Their flood below;
And in the flooded subterranean hall
        The level tables shift and fall—
                No cates, no glow
Of roses; but the flood and flowers and men
        Are drenched and whelmed and then
                Sink or expire.
Silent the sodden flowers, but the men shriek,
        As Nilus and my Aznac wreak
                The anger dire

110

That is as Nile in flood within my soul,
    That is as Aznac, built and whole
        Within my breast,
That must absorb, kill and obliterate,
    With rich capacities of hate,
        Those I detest."

She laid her face upon the marble ledge:
The gurgle ceased to chafe the river's edge;
And the great Palace held the bodies tight
Of those who murdered Papi in the night.

She lifted up her face, with wearied eyes,
Priestess of unavailing sacrifice.
The stars looked weary back into her eyes.
She listened . . . fain to hear from living cries.
The water hummed beside a crocodile:
And Aznac threw its shadow on the Nile.

T1276   A single draft survives in Henry's hand (OWQ 70-7), written probably
about 1906; published DEDICATED, DDD 111-5. Nitocris is thought to
have been a Queen of Egypt in her own right, possibly the last 6th
Dynasty ruler (Old Kingdom c 2181 BC), but archaeological evidence is tenuous.
Henry's poem seems based on an account in Herodotus's *Histories*, Book II ¶100:
"by way of revenge for her brother, who had been king and slain by his subjects
before they made her queen... She built a spacious hall under ground and... gave a
great feast there and invited all those whom she knew were most concerned in the
death of her brother; and as they feasted she let the river run in upon them through
a secret waterway of great size... when she had accomplished this deed she threw
herself in a room filled with ashes" (Harry Carter translation, OUP). Also known as
Rhodopis, courtesan and mythical builder of the third pyramid at Giza, she may yet
be seen off Kensington Gore in London, seated holding a pyramid (and overlooked
suspiciously by Cheops), on the NW podial frieze of the Albert Memorial.

Aznac:	Presumably Nitocris's great Palace on the Nile.
cheeks of roses:	Manetho described her as "braver than all the men of her time, the most beautiful of all the women, fair-skinned with red cheeks". (ICT: Hence probably *Rhodopis*).
Papi:	Perhaps another spelling for Pepi; there were two previous 6th Dynasty Pharaohs called Pepi, the last being her father-in-law.
murdered:	Teti, the father of Pepi I, is said to have been killed by his palace guards; but this Pharaoh cannot have been her literal brother.
She laid her face:	Ricketts wrote from Cairo in January 1911: 'The Museum owns the Sarcophagus, not the mummy, of Nitocris. She reclines in granite upon her granite bed, the expression on her face points to her knowledge that the enemies she drowned are unrepresented in the Museum" (OZF 39).

But if our love be dying let it die
As the rose shedding secretly,
Or as a noble music's pause:
Let it move rhythmic as the laws
Of the sea's ebb, or the sun's ritual
When sovereignly he dies:
Then let a mourner rise and three times call
Upon our love, and the long echoes fall.

T1287   The three autographs, all in Michael's hand, agree in the footnote date
         After midnight Saturday Sept 15 1906 (ZJV 168b). There is no title, even
         in WILD HONEY, WDH 24. The previous November Michael had received
some unwelcome news 'Francis is engaged... makes a void where there has been
greenness' (ZJT 121a sa OCA 124a). She could hardly have expected him to hang
around for ever, he was already 44 (she had probably had her last chance in 1902,
T1087-8); but when he eventually married Beatrice Wade that April she must have
felt especially desolate (ZJV 74-5). In August Michael Field was visiting the Ryans in
Ireland for the first time; Amy played a Chopin waltz which set off Henry into
nostalgic memories of Stoke Green some twenty years before. 'Michael with folded
perfect hands on her velvet lap, Francis shadowing his brows opposite to her— his
eyes taking the music as the expression of his youthful passion for her...' (ZJV 162a).
Michael took up this motive, *In an old music I have found your face*— (T1286) within
days, but it was not until September that she wrote this resonant piece, and then an
extended version (T1290) of T1286. The link is clear in the Journal: 'Francis just
married & signing himself in his still fate-touched letters to Michael "Yours
affectionately" instead of "Your own" of the last letter before marriage!' (H ZJV 162b).
In a further splendidly bitchy passage, Henry remarks: 'there is nothing so
phantasmal as to see the images of the men one has moved; & then sharply realise
the present & the 'cattle-wives' too many have settled in the fields with, where there is
grass & comfort' (ZJV 163a). Without access to the Journal, interpretation of the
personae of the poem is well-nigh impossible; the truth is only now apparent. Little
wonder then that Mary Sturgeon assumed this was Henry rejecting Berenson, highly
commendable though this would have been— alas, she would have jumped at the
Palmer-worm (T0678,1073), given half a chance (FMS 86). Elizabeth Selden added a
further gloss to this " ... episode in Edith Cooper's life which might have broken the
companionship. For a time she contemplated marriage, and Katherine Bradley
generously offered to step aside, as expressed in the poem" (AES 198). Even so, this
interpretation is psychologically nearer the truth for both women— '... if the great
Lord Love himself should ever come to you— to him I will freely give you' (Michael in
a letter to Henry in 1885, OCA 122). Poor Beatrice was not easily forgiven.

three times: See the note *sacred number* to T0295.

Descendit ad Inferos

Thou risest in great quiet from Thy bed:
It may be that Thou hast one tear to shed
Over the Roman guard that slumbereth.
Nor drawn back to the house that numbereth
Thy Mother, Thy Beloved; nor tempted where
Peter is lying in profound nightmare,
And can by no means wake till the cock crow,
Thou bendest not where in the Eastern blow
Of summer-dawning clouds there is delight,
Where as at first God says 'Let there be light'—
As a gray pilgrim, russet thou dost go,
Sprinkling the bloodless land of Shadows wide
From hands that drip; for they were crucified.

T1341   Known from a single manuscript in the Fortey cache, an undated autograph in the hand of Henry (YFC 9b); there is no good reason to suspect it is not her work, especially since it has a Latin title. In August 1907 they had been visited by Emily Fortey (MFC 58), a friend of the Ryans— 'a soul full of fervour and kindness' (OCP 38o); she was to figure increasingly in their lives, and later to preserve MSS. which might otherwise have been destroyed. *Descendit ad Inferos* is the first poem in a notebook with the inside cover label of an Edinburgh stationer; dated poems following run mostly consecutively from October 1907 to April 1908. It is not unlikely the book was bought September 1907 when Michael Field was on a visit to Scotland; and this could date the poem at Autumn 1907. In the Spring of that same year they had been accepted into the Roman Catholic Church, Henry leading and Michael meekly following (ZJW 54b, FCR 6). This was dramatically to restrict their subject matter, but not their palette; there were a few splendid final pictures still to paint. The "Harrowing of Hell" myth can be traced back to c 1000; Christ is supposed to have rescued the souls of the 'noble pagans', who could hardly be damned for denying him, having predated him. This also conveniently filled in a day's gap between entombment and resurrection.

Descendit ad Inferos:	He descended into Hell (Apostles' Creed, but not the Nicaean).
Roman guard:	Matthew XXVII 64-5
house that numbereth :	presumably Zebedee's (John XIX 26-7) sa T1445
Thy Beloved:	John the Divine (son of Zebedee, Matthew IV 21)
cock crow:	Matthew XXVI 74-5
Let there be light:	Genesis I 3
land of Shadows:	'In pagente sett out the harrowinge of helle' (Chester Plays 1450). sa T0594,1412,655

113

More secret art thou than a secret thing
That peers upon the surface of the sea,
And re-appears, re-volting instantly;
Or, as some traveller's remembering
Of shade, or light in cleft, or sudden spring
Of unseen fount, or movement from a tree.
If for a moment thou dost pause by me
It is a token, an admonishing.
Thou canst not gauge the apparition sent,
Nor of what computation it befell;
Nor wherefore thou must pause with such intent
And measured steps a furlong from the well,
St. Hubert's lovely stag of breathing eyes,
Amid his antlers God in sacrifice.

T1373   An untitled italian sonnet written by Henry, 'My Sonnet— the first in <u>Wilder Honey</u>' (H ZJY 89b), in early May 1908; WILD HONEY had been published the previous December. There is one other autograph, in Michael's hand in one of her 'Scribble Books' (YFE 17b). The poem was finally printed in the *A Rank of Osiers* section of THE WATTLEFOLD (TWF 73), by Emily Fortey. Her published version has an apparently arbitrary typographic layout, including an 8,6 split at the octave, and minor punctuation differences; it carries a footnote date *May, 1908*. It is quite probable she was working from a third autograph now lost, and the version is almost certainly equally valid. What is most interesting, is that this should be a sonnet by Henry, a rarity indeed; its numinous nature culminates in an astonishing image.

re-volting: Turning back; the TWF version omits both hyphens where they occur in this verse. In Henry's autograph the verse begins *Then* not *And*.

St. Hubert: Henry seems to have had a particular interest in Hubert (ZJG 5a,ZKA 59b). According to the legend, Hubert was a nobleman who, while hunting on Good Friday in the Forest of Freyr (SE Belgium) in 683, had a vision of a crucifix between the antlers of the stag he was pursuing; the experience changed his life, and he eventually became the first bishop of Liège. The story seems a make over from an earlier tale of the much less fortunate Placidus, a general in the Roman army under Trajan and Hadrian ca 100. After an identical experience a 'divine' voice informed him he would 'suffer much'. This proved to be no understatement. He was baptised Eustachius, and for refusing to sacrifice to the Roman gods, he and his family were roasted alive inside a brass bull. Both men for obvious reasons are patron saints of venery; the rest, including the *Jägermeister* trademark, is all too predictable.

To a Cuckoo, interrupting prayer

Cuckoo, thou comest unawares,
As with a question to my prayers;
Full am I of my soul's annoy—
And thou, indifferent in joy,
Dost toss thy voice as if a ball,
Dost chase, and fling and let it fall.
Tempted am I to thy free-faring:
Cuckoo, but there is no comparing!
The Apple hung upon the bough
When, renegade from Eden, thou
To thy freebooter's life broke loose.
My teeth have pressed against the juice,
The foaming juice of sin's delight.
Christ my offences doth requite;
He died upon the Cross for these—
To win back my Hesperides:
And I remain upon my knees.

T1375   Written by Michael, almost certainly in May 1908. Neither of the two
        autographs has a year indicated, but the poem was published in issue
        #1881 of *The Academy* for 23 May 1908, and there is a direct reference
to the trigger event in a letter to Amy of about this time: "I was praying in the early
morn— & lo the Cuckoo— heard for the 1st time" (OCT 36r). One of the two Fortey
manuscripts has a footnote *May—ended May 9th* (YFE 16b). Two related letters OCR
182,6o refer to the JAC appearance, as does a Journal entry for June 1908 (ZJY
103b). A truly delightful poem, it is not surprising it was singled out for praise by both
Salter and Ricketts (ZKD 31a,45a) when eventually published as the opening poem
of *Sward* in MYSTIC TREES, MCT 85 in 1913. Other earlier Cuckoo poems include
T0395 and T0916, but the layers of reference in this text are particularly subtle.

Apple: Genesis II 17, III 6
freebooter: Pirate; probably a reference to its life at the expense of other birds.
Hesperides: An allusion to the far Western orchard with its tree bearing golden
            apples, that Gaea gave to Hera on her marriage to Zeus; Zeus
            courted Hera, his twin sister, disguised as a cuckoo. The Hesperides,
            the clear-voiced 'Daughters of Evening', guard this pleasanter, less
            guilt-fraught Eden, abetted by the dragon Ladon.

Giving place—

Thou art not, though thy hawthorns on the air
Spread rich, thy lilacs sweeping everywhere
      Persia's fine way
      Superbly gray,
Though thy laburnums drop— thou art not there,
      There is no May.

It is the June, the lovely June concealed,
And all her beauties treasured that will yield
      Themselves, how soon!
      My senses swoon;
Where the white umbels blow across the field
      There must be June.

T1378   A single autograph survives in Michael's hand, dated May 21st (YFD 28b).
To this an unknown hand (probably Emily Fortey's) has added the year
1908. This seems to be correct, as the poem was published in *The
Academy* 13 June 1908 (#1884, OYT 228) with the full date 21 May 1908. Emily
included the piece in *A Rank of Osiers* in THE WATTLEFOLD, TWF 52. Her text has
variant punctuation, with the same full date as a footnote.

hawthorns: See the note to T0446.
gray: The TWF text reads *grey*.
umbels: Parasol-like inflorescences typical of the carrot and hemlock family, in
this case possibly hogweed *Heracleum*, or cow-parsley *Anthriscus*.
June: In a Journal entry for 01 June 1908, Henry comments 'How June
begins— just the May getting out of her depth!' (ZJY 97b). Which
shows yet again, assuming the piece to be Michael's, the closeness of
their thought processes. Or as Henry herself was to write in August
1910, 'Is not Michael Field one soul?' (ZKA 120a)

Fregit

On the night of dedication
Of Thyself as our oblation,
Christ, Belovèd, Thou didst take
In Thy very hands and break. . . .

O my God, there is the hiss of doom
When new-glowing flowers are snapt in bloom;
When shivered, as a little thunder-cloud,
A vase splits on the floor its brilliance loud;
Or lightning strikes a willow-tree with gash
Cloven for death in a resounded crash;
And I have heard that one who could betray
His country and yet face the breadth of day,
Bowed himself, weeping, but to hear his sword
Broken before him, as his sin's award.
These were broken; Thou didst break. . . .

Thou the Flower that Heaven did make
Of our race the crown of light;
Thou the Vase of Chrysolite
Into which God's balm doth flow;
Thou the Willow hung with woe
Of our exile harps; Thou Sword
Of the Everlasting Word—
Thou, betrayed, Thyself didst break
Thy own Body for our sake:
Thy own Body Thou didst take
In Thy holy hands— and break.

T1386   Known only from POEMS OF ADORATION, PAD 5. This poem by Henry
cannot be dated exactly, but was most probably written June/July 1908. At
Corpus Christi, 18 June, she writes to her sister 'a poem came to me'
(OCS 30o), and by July 01 'Michael asks me to read my poem "Fregit"' (ZJY 118b).

Fregit: Broke. I Corinthians XI 24 'this is my body, which is broken for
you'; the Vulgate text may be Mark XIV 22: *accepit Jesus panem: et
benidicens fregit, et dedit eis et ait: Sumite, hoc est corpus meum.*
Chrysolite: A golden yellow variety of olivine sa Othello V ii 144, and T1713.
harps: We hanged our harps upon the willows... (Psalm 137, 2).

A College Song

Father Placide takes the roses—
And distributes them in peace:
Peacefully the people stand,
Take the roses, kiss his hand,
And depart in peace.

Father Prior takes the roses,
And among them seeks for one—
But the knotted thorns withstand:
From the thicket in his hand
Can he single one?

Father Placide leaves no strewing
Of the roses on the floor:
To the people, as they come,
White & blush, & bleeding flame—
And no strewing on the floor.

Father Prior leaves a strewing
Of great petals at his feet,
Wrestlings, droppings, lovely drops,
And the wrestled leaves in crops
Left behind the eager feet.

Father Placide, as is fitted,
Leaves us undisturbed & good:
There were roses at command,
There was no election planned,
As the lot falls it is good

Oh, it is an eagle's litter,
Father Prior, where you stood!

T1460 Among letters written 1908-9 to Amy, this single undated autograph is in
Michael's hand (OCS 85o); the piece is more likely to be Michael's than
Henry's. There are intrusive Roman numerals at stanzas II-V which serve
no justifiable purpose; they have accordingly been omitted. The poem can be dated

Holy Communion

In the Beginning— and in me,
Flesh of my flesh, O Deity,
    Bone of my bone;
    In me alone
Create, as if on Thy sixth day,
I, of frail breath and clay,
Were yet one seed with Thee,
Engendering Trinity!

My Lord, the honour of great fear
To be Thy teeming *fiat* here;
    In blood and will
    Urged to fulfil
Thy rounded motion of behest;
One with Thy power and blest
To act by aim and right
Of Thy prevenient might!

with some confidence to early October 1909 (envelope franked 12 Oct 1909 at OCS 86o); it relates directly to a Journal entry by Henry for 'Rosary Sunday', 03 October 1909: 'At High Mass the roses in their soft cushions of bloom are blessed at the altar & then Fr Placide & Fr Prior distribute them to the people as they kneel' (ZJZ 158ab). October 7 would be the calendar Feast Day of the Rosary.

College: The scene was Holy Cross, the Dominican Priory at Leicester.
Placide: Placid (sic) Conway was the SubPrior, unflatteringly described by Henry as 'a sanctified & cultured buffoon' (ZJZ 181b sa 188a). The play on his name throughout stanza 1 is no doubt intentional.
Father Prior: Vincent McNabb had been appointed the previous year.
a strewing: 'The claws of the White Eagle have mangled the blooms' (H ZJZ 159a). McNabb (Michael's austere confessor, aka 'the elegant wasp') had early on been so-named by Michael Field, for his aquiline authoritarianism; he was obviously cack-handed with it.

T1480   A mystical poem, almost certainly by Henry (sa second note to T1595), published in POEMS OF ADORATION, PAD 8. In the absence of an autograph and any detected local or Journal reference, the date of composition (within a range 1907-11) is problematic.

sixth day: Creation myth, Genesis I 24-31.
prevenient: 'Coming before'; predisposing (through grace) to compliance.

Penance

I would make offering to appease!
Great creatures, kneeling on their knees,
   Burdening down mountain-rocks
   Stupendous in their blocks—
I would toil, pilgrim to my God, as these;
     Who travel in their mass,
     Through their mountain-pass.
I would bring magnitude to Thee,
     Who art Infinity:
My God, in penance I would pant,
     As the devoted Elephant,
Who, in his bulk he hath,
Bows down and up, to keep his path.

T1497   Known from three autographs, all in Michael's hand: an early draft, untitled and undated (ORM 30), and two others dated *Quinquagesima Sunday*. That January of 1910 Death had again visited Michael Field. Amy, worn out by good works among the Irish poor, fell sick with influenza and rapidly succumbed to a fatal pneumonia; she died on the 22nd and her body was shipped back to England, accompanied by John and "Emily the strong". One of the *Penance* autographs is a Blackfriars manuscript, backed by another poem T1518 dated 11 April 1910 (YSQ BKF 7.60); the other is within a sequence of dated poems for 1910 (OWN 6b). Quinquagesima Sunday for 1910 was February 06, so the poem was written nine days after the burial of Amy Ryan at St. Mary Magdalen RC Cemetery at Mortlake; the Journal was silent the whole of this month.The poem was eventually printed, with what appears as a clumsy and arbitrary typographic justification, in a subgroup *The First Day* in MYSTIC TREES, MCT 128. The more reasonable layout given here is that of the Blackfriars manuscript.

blocks: The rhyme with *rocks*, also used in T1524, might conceivably indicate a contribution by Michael in the latter poem (v8).

Through :   The Blackfriars manuscript possibly reads *Thorough*, rhythmically a more interesting scansion.

Elephant: Ricketts, in a letter to Michael about MYSTIC TREES, dated 14 May 1913: '... I dispute your theology and some of your naughty rhymes, so naughty that they are sometimes nice, like the elephant who rhymes with pant...' (ZKD 45a, VCR 30). It is just possible the poem relates to a drawing.

Crying out

In the Orient heat He stands—
Heat that makes the palm-trees dim,
Palms that do not shelter Him,
As under the fierce blue He stands with outstretched hands.

As a lizard of the rocks,
Under furnace-sun He stays;
Earth beneath Him in a daze
Is faint and trembling, spite of rocks, in shadeless blocks.

He among them mid the blue,
With a mouth wide open held,
As a lion-fountain welled
Under the spaciousness of blue, the heat throbs through.

Wide His mouth as lion's, set
Wide for waters of a fount!
Through them words of challenge mount,
Great words that cry through them, wide-set, where men
          have met.

"Ye the thirsty come to Me!"
So He cries with lion-roar:
"Ye will thirst not any more.
Come!" and He stands for all to see, and offers free.

Jesus, in the Eastern sun,
A strange prophet with His cry!
While the folk are passing by,
And clack their tongues, nor will they run where thirst is done.

T1524 This piece was published in POEMS OF ADORATION, PAD 81-2; the single
         known autograph OWN 31-2 is undated (and untitled), but falls within a
         chronologically consistent group April through May 1910. It is possible the
draft was written that April during their stay at Wincanton, where they 'slept in a bed
once inhabited by Queen Victoria' (M ZKA 60b). Authorship is more problematic.
Metrically inept (especially the lumpen-footed final verse of each stanza), the piece is
most memorable for its extraordinary central image based on John IV 14 (sa
T0798,1508). *Crying out* is marginally more likely to be Henry's work; in which case
it is possible the OWN draft is a fair copy in Michael's hand (but sa T1497).

Mischief

I travelled a forest
Of ancient root
With one who was not pagan with the flowers,
And therefore was afraid; this they knew well
And quickened in his eyes delicious powers
As they assailed him, hostile in their showers
Of glint & poignant balsam. In the spell
The trees grew gentle & immeasurable
The worth of things was changed amid the trees
Terror was passing into headlong ease
And sighs & lights were lit about the brain.
When we were on the open road again
He tossed into the air, as one set free,
His cap, & tried to sing of liberty,
And hailed the exit to the highway route
But looking back— it was so strange a thing
That, looking back, just as I saw him stand
I saw how there remained within his hand
Mint, & a branch of oak-leaves silvering,
And a pagoda of the self-heal's fruit.

T1552 This sketch is known from two autographs, one in Michael's hand, undated
(once again she makes use of a prose entry made in the Journal by Henry);
this is the text given here (OWN 67b). The other, in the hand of Emily
Fortey, shows several small differences, including the run on of verse one into verse
two (OYR 30o). It is dated August 1910; there is no reason to dispute this. The poem
is a record of a coach outing with Fitzgibbon 15 August 1910, into the forest near
Boulogne. This was to be the last time they left England.

one who was not pagan:	Gerald Fitzgibbon ("Gosscannon") was Henry's confessor (sa T1553, MFC).
His cap:	'He tosses up his cap.... in Gossie's hand the mint I had gathered & given him, a spray of little silver oak leaves & the pagoda of the self-heal's fruit' H ZKA 131-3
self-heal:	*Prunella vulgaris*, one of the mint family (Labiatae); decoctions are used in gargles for sore mouth or throat.

Loved, on a sudden thou didst come to me
On our own doorstep, still I see thee stand
In thy bleared welcome, with the grim command
From Heaven that we must sever presently;
And no farewell was in the misery . . .
So you condemned me; did not understand
O lovely and gay-coloured tulip-land,
I would not break on thee my wrathful sea;
    Back to the flood-gates, firm to my defence—
So hard, as thou complainest, so apart;
But had I not held tight from thee my sense,
My memory, my will against my heart,
But one defeat, the rupture of one sigh
How little of the world had been left dry!

T1595   An untitled italian sonnet in Michael's hand dated 19 April 1911,
published posthumously in the group *The Fall of the Leaf*, THE
WATTLEFOLD, TWF 186; the date, also appended in the published
text, is further confirmed by the autograph footnote *Feast of St Elphage* (OWN 87).
On 14 November 1910 Henry had recorded in the Journal 'I cannot eat; I don't
remember ever feeling more deadly-deep in sickness' (ZKA 221a); on 06 February
1911 her doctor discovered bowel cancer. Michael was faced with this news when
she returned home; to this was added the pain of Henry's incomprehension of her
own stoicism. The metaphor of inundation in the poem vividly conveys Michael's
suppressed grief (an early draft, YFE 46, attempted the trope of an avalanche).

own doorstep: 'Henry told me.... at once, suddenly, letting me in at the door— the
Doctor had seen her while I was out' (M ZKB 22b).
we must sever: 'flesh of one flesh in our imaginations— bone of one bone in our
common life.... how infinitely distant from the love I have for her
are all, even the tenderest other loves' (H ZKB 19b cf v2-3 T1480).
tulip-land: Their tulips had been a special delight the previous May (ZKA
95,6,8a); it may have been a memory of these that finally clinched
the Netherlands image central to the poem.
so hard: The 'psychic' Henry could be astonishingly obtuse where it really
mattered; Michael understood the importance of strength in crisis
(ZKA 50b). When Henry might have died in the Dresden fever
hospital in August 1891, Michael wrote: 'I have not shed a tear—
scarcely, through all the biting trouble of this week. But my heart is
thickly inscribed as an Egyptian tomb' (ZJD 97a).

Caput tuum ut Carmelus

I watch the arch of her head,
As she turns away from me . . .
I would I were with the dead,
Drowned with the dead at sea,
All the waves rocking over me!

As St. Peter turned and fled
From the Lord, because of sin,
I look on that lovely head;
And its majesty doth win
Grief in my heart as for sin.

Oh, what can Death have to do
With a curve that is drawn so fine,
With a curve that is drawn as true
As the mountain's crescent line? . . .
Let me be hid where the dust falls fine!

T1603   Two autographs exist, a preliminary draft (YFE 56b), untitled and undated;
and a fair copy dated 23 May 1911 (OWN 94b). It was printed in MYSTIC
TREES, MCT 146, in a subgroup titled *A Little While*, and was one of the
poems singled out for mention by Edwin Essex. He met Michael Field at St. Thomas's
Priory, Hawkesyard, some two months after the piece was written; he remembered
how 'Miss Bradley would sit there, almost pontifical in dignity, jealously watchful of
her niece's requirements, instantly solicitous' (JCM 1931 #8, 242-3)

Caput tuum:	*Thine head upon thee is like Carmel.* A quotation from the Vulgate *Canticum Canticorum* (Song of Songs) VII 5. Carmel in Palestine is a range of forested hills proverbial for its orchards and gardens.
St. Peter:	Matthew XXVI 74-5
mountain:	Mount Carmel, a 'high place' from antiquity, forms a promontory onto the Mediterranean coast above Haifa.
crescent:	Both autographs read *cresset,* a much more striking image, which brings to mind the lines from *Her Profile* (T1215):

a radiance swims/ From candles lit beyond that face of hers

But the printed text must be respected, even though in those last
days such a slippery error could well have escaped Michael's notice.

To Columbines

I behold you in a dance
Of most plastic circumstance—
Lying, folded on the air,
Sprinkled, dropping everywhere,
Bud and beacon, spur and trail,
Buoyant on your stalks ye sail,
Feigning every dent and dip
Of the swallow and the ship,
Caught up as the foam at play,
Yet majestic in your play,
Motionless or high or low,
Up and down the air ye flow.

Not a glance is upward sent
To the swaying firmament,
All your looks that nod and bound
Have their centre on the ground,
While the knot of spurry things
That must be your folded wings
Is above your heads arrayed
As an umbel or a shade;
Thus ye stand in poise most keen,
Something mystical, between
Nun and gamester, in your mien!
And sweet truth the answer gives
That ye are Contemplatives.

T1605   First printed in *A Rank of Osiers*, THE WATTLEFOLD, TWF 89. Two
autographs exist, both in Michael's hand; one is dated 29 May 1911
(OWN 96-7) in agreement with the footnote *1911* in THE WATTLEFOLD.
The other autograph, in a Fortey cache manuscript, consists of working sketches for
stanza two only; this is titled *Contemplatives* (YFE 57ab). In July Michael confided to
the Journal her concern that 'Dominicans neglect Contemplation' (ZKB 111b).   sa
T1704,7

behold: TWF has *beheld*, which must be a printer's (or Miss Fortey's) error.
folded wings: Columbines (*Aquilegia*) are so-called, from a fanciful resemblance
to a cluster of doves.

Too late

"O Virgins, very lovely in your troop,
O Virgins very lovely, very white,
How is it that your lilies droop?
How is it that the lamps you bear are not alight?

Why are you bending downward from the hill?
Bright is it on the hill as for a feast."
Trembling they sped as to fulfil
Some grievous prophecy; nor heeded me the least.

Downward they passed . . . Oh, they were very fair,
But stricken as the frosted leaves to doom!
Their eyes I saw . . . Bright with despair
Their eyes, and very lamps to light them to their doom.

Full were their looks of love and sorrowing
As they passed by me, shaking out a spell
Of sighs, of balms. And is it such a thing
Can be, that they were hurrying to Hell?

T1645   The single autograph, in Michael's hand, is untitled and undated (OWN
109b); but it lies between poems separately dated January 1912
(T1644,6). It was printed in the subgroup *Sward* in MYSTIC TREES, MCT
100. The story is the familiar one of Matthew XXV 1-13, and the poem pleased both
Sturge Moore (ZKD 75a) and Ricketts (ZKD 45a). In a letter from Ricketts to Michael
dated 14 May 1913 he wrote: "You are much more with the Naughty Virgins who
ran after cuckoos (*ICT: probably a reference to T1375*) and red currants. I like your
poem about them, 'Too Late', though I dispute your theology..." (VCR 30).

lamps: Michael wrote to John Gray in 1907, probably sometime in April,
'sometimes deliberately I have turned my lamp upside down to be sure
not a drop of oil was left in it' (ZJW 221a).   sa T1140

After Mass

Lovingly I turn me down
From this church, St. Philip's crown,
To the leafy street where dwell
    The good folk of Arundel.

Lovingly I look between
Roof and roof, to meadows green,
To the cattle by the wall,
To the place where sea-birds call,

Where the sky more closely dips,
And perchance, there may be ships:
God have pity on us all!

T1662   Written by Michael in July 1912, and published in the subgroup *Sward* in
MYSTIC TREES, MCT 143. An autograph in Michael's hand exists (dated 27
July 1912); this runs on stanzas 2 and 3, and was sent in a letter to
McNabb (YSQ BKF 7.64o, sa ZKC 104b).

By this time Henry's illness was advanced, and the burden on Michael become
almost intolerable. The previous October Ricketts had been 'rather shocked at the
weariness & pain of Michael's face' (ZKB 147), and by November she was confessing
to the Journal 'I am broken, broken on the wheel. Henry cannot understand this.'
(ZKB 153a, sa T0507). In March 1912 she broke her right wrist (ZKC 24-6), but both
were overjoyed to receive a first published copy of POEMS OF ADORATION in April,
'We who had feared the event would find us parted' (H ZKC 44b). July saw them,
intrepid as ever, departing by car for a six-week holiday in Arundel (sa T1663) in a
vicarage with five cats. This was to be Henry's last idyllically happy time, not least
perhaps because of visits by Berenson. Of one such she wrote 'I am too weak to talk
long— mostly he talks to Michael, while I watch the face that launched all the ships
in the harbour of my passion years ago & sent them voyaging among dreams &
sorrows' (ZKC 73b). She was indeed too weak to venture out of the vicarage, and
this is the background of Michael's poem. Its child-like directness leaves so much
unsaid. Mary Sturgeon, commenting on the poem, records "Michael said, in a letter
to a friend, *Mystic Trees* is for the young'; and one perceives the truth of that... a
certain kind of child would delight in them". She wondered if Michael herself realised
"how she had in them recaptured her own youth and its lyrical fervour" (FMS 108-10
ICT: See for example T0095). Yet as Sturgeon herself recognised, there is a grief
and experience here, a technical skill, which belie the outward simplicity of form.

place: The autograph reads *space*. 'I offer you, Father, a tiny Sketch of this
Arundel— If only it were not so infested of heretics!' (M YSQ BKF 7.64r).

My Summer

Jesus, hanging on a Tree,
Thou hast heard a cry from me;
Not that sins of mine may fall
To the ground, as stained leaves fall,
From Thy awful Tree-trunk tall:
But a cry burst up to Thee
From pain long borne and from long weariness:
"O Jesus, from Thy Tree,
Grant me some leaves to see,
Some leaves this summer, that will bless
My eyes this summer with their play;
Their motions or their stillness in the day,
Their motions or their stillness in the night;
The colours of their play,
The froth upon the breeze of their delight."

I gaze upon the gold of beechen leaves,
So gold, wherre the shade heaves
Its dark against the deer, exposed, sun-red;
        And Paradise is spread—
By light of beech-trees, as a visiting dream,
That thrills to joy, with each unearthly gleam—
Down slopes, up valleys of the beechen groves,
Round little hidden by-ways the doe loves.
I greet the freshness round the flickered wings
By tiny, sheltering things,
That love the leaves as I;
Yea, hear the many sudden springs
Of breeze, that jet from clumps and run about
Among the branches, fountains in a rout,
That run and ripple and then cease,
And then all die,
Lulled down to peace.

I hear the wind,
Whose birthplace none can find,
Washing the leaves as with the salt of waves;
And making for itself green caves

To roar into, retreat from, and distress
With moaning loneliness.
I hear the rain fall with a silver chink
Over each tree's wind-ruffled brink;
I hear it spend its silver wealth and sigh
          Most mournfully;
Then, prodigal, once more the silver hoard
Chinks on the verduous foliage adored.
O Jesus, hanging on a leafless Tree,
What succour Thou hast sent to me
From Thy dire boughs, O Weary One,
          O Love, in utter pain!
Lo, what Thy sufferer prayed of Thee is done;
And I am girt with beech-leaves in the sun,
          With beech-trees in the rain.

O Jesus, hanging on the Tree of Trees,
          How bountiful the ease
And pleasure Thou dost grant from Holy Rood—
          To let the forest flow
About my Cross; to let its music hum
Round beams, to Thee stone-dumb;
To let its many waves, that blow
And waver in the wind, fall soft
And sun-lit for me, while aloft
Thou hangest naked on a naked Tree,
          Lord of the stricken Wood!

T1663   A text known only from *Hawkesyard Review* V5 #15 pp 155-6; this is the
          original version of Henry's poem, probably written in Autumn 1912.
On 4 July Michael Field had taken a six week summer break at Arundel
which seems to have been organised by the Berensons; 'How I longed for leaves....
The gracious reply to my sick yearning has been Arundel of the beeches' (9 August
ZKC 95b). But it was (apparently) not written at Arundel: 'I have not written one word
of poetry' (15 August ZKC 104b).   The poem appeared in the Midsummer 1913
Hawkesyard Review, and was praised by Ricketts (ZKD 57a). On a later visit however
'He would have <u>My Summer</u> shorter and in the night watches I shorten it' (ZKD
59a,OZF 113); it was this diminished version T1696 which was published
posthumously in THE WATTLEFOLD, TWF 48-9. One suspects that Ricketts, sensitive
to Henry's suffering, and on record as 'detesting' religious poetry (ZKC 48b), found
its elaboration painful; yet it is essentially in its murmurous and mimetic extent that
the hypnotic power of the piece lies. Surely on this occasion, as on another, he was
wrong (cf T1128).

Descendit

Souls that are bowed before Thy Altar-stone
    Each one alone
And yet in crowd, like dark trees of a grove—
    Christ, in Thy love,
Let fall Thy holy Wafers as small spots
    Of sun through plots
Of forest-shadow: penetrating, fall
    Thy life on all,
With blessed radiance of parted sun
    Shed on each one,
Keen little circles of Thy Godhead's Light
    Snatched by twilight!
Thy forest shall rejoice that bows so dull
    O Beautiful;
The roundlets and the wheels of Thy bright Power
    Become our Dower!

T1666   A poem known only from its inclusion in THE WATTLEFOLD, TWF 8. Emily
Fortey placed it in her subgroup *Corn and Vines*, with a footnote *1912*.
    There seems little reason, in the absence of an autograph or any other
leaders, to dispute this attribution. The poem has all the marks of Henry the mystic,
and may well relate to her ecstatic time in the forest at Arundel (sa T1663). A
reasonable assumption for date of composition is therefore August 1912.

Descendit: Almost certainly a Missal fragment from the Nicæan Creed: *Qui propter
nos homines, et propter nostram salutem, descendit de cælis;* Who for
us men, and for our salvation, came down from heaven.
Wafers: The imaginative leap here is perhaps one of Henry's finest, and is
reminiscent of her use of the blossom-drift trope in T1060. In another
poem (T1653) she wrote of the Eucharist host as a white moon, which
shows an interesting link with pagan concepts of Artemis and Selene.
roundlets: Little circles or discs
Dower: A word sometimes used in the sense of a marriage-gift to a wife, and so
presumably an allusion to the popular conceit of Christ as the
'Bridegroom'.

The Open Air

As I pass,
Drawing up the hill from Mass,
   Lo, I gather
Leaves of plumèd yarrow,
And rose-bindweed in a braid
For one drooping in the shade
Where the sweet flowers are not made;
   And the butterfly
Never, never thrilleth by.

T1670   In September 1912 there was a last visit together to their beloved Rottingdean, the scene since 1901 of so many writing holidays, at work on the final group of dramas. They seem to have been there almost the whole month. 'This little place,' Henry had once recorded, 'is the Lourdes of the Imagination— it loses all its ailments, walks & sings' (ZJS 97a). The present poem was probably written there by Michael on 22 September. For that day (a Sunday), Henry notes in the Journal 'My Beloved writes two very short but very mature poems on our bit of waste ground' (ZKC 125a). The directness and simplicity, and the pathos, recall those features of T1662; like it, the piece was eventually published in the subgroup *Sword* in MYSTIC TREES, MCT 140. In 1914 the *Hawkesyard Review* reprinted it in the March issue (JHR V6 #17 pp 142-3), and Michael kept the cutting in the Journal for that final year (ZKE 19b).

yarrow: Mentioned again in T1671 (the second of the 'two very short... poems'), which more specifically refers to:

          a plot of chalky ground,
          Little villas dotted round;
          On a sea-worn waste

bindweed: See the note to T0294.

the shade: There is no evidence that Henry ventured out of doors; the last time she walked on the Downs had been the previous October (ZKB 148).

Qui Renovat Juventutem Meam

Make me grow young again,
Grow young enough to die,
That, in a joy unseared of pain,
I may my Lover, loved, attain,
    With that fresh sigh
    Eternity
Gives to the young to breathe about the heart,
Until their trust in youth-time shall depart.

Let me be young as when
To die was past my thought:
And Earth with straight, immortal men,
And women deathless to my ken,
    Cast fear to naught!
    Let Faith be fraught,
My Bridegroom, with such gallant love, its range
Simply surpasses every halt of Change!

Let me come to Thee young,
When Thou dost challenge *Come !*
With all my marvelling dreams unsung,
Their promise by first passion stung,
    Though chary, dumb . . .
    Thou callest *Come !*
Let me rush to Thee when I pass,
Keen as a child across the grass!

T1672   It is possible to trace three stages in the evolution of this poem, the two
extant Blackfriars autographs, both in Henry's hand, and the final
published version in the subgroup *Sward* of MYSTIC TREES, MCT 119.
That the work is Henry's cannot be questioned. She seems to have written it in
September 1912, perhaps in response to a remark by McNabb on the need to 'be a
child again' (ZKC 126a). She certainly discussed it with him (ZKC 131b). The poem is

unusual in having been printed in MYSTIC TREES, since this was the book consisting almost entirely of Michael's poems. Henry recorded its inclusion 'on my behalf' in June 1913 (ZKD 52a, sa 39b); her own religious collection POEMS OF ADORATION having already been published in April 1912, before the poem was written. The original working draft (YSN BKF 4.21) is untitled, but the fair copy (YSQ BKF 7.68) is headed *Qui Laetificat Juventutem Meam*; this Missal phrase is taken from the opening antiphon response of the catechumen part of the Mass:

> *Introibo ad altare Dei*
> *Ad Deum qui lætificat juventutem meam.*

> I will go in unto the altar of God
> Unto God, who giveth joy to my youth.

On publication, the new title *Qui Renovat Juventutem Meam* (Who renews my youth) was probably chosen as more appropriate to the theme. At this time too one of the stanzas, the second in the original set of four, was discarded:

> Let me be young once more,
> And all my weakness fling,
> Invincible, upon that store
> Of strength in Him, His Saints adore,
> His Angels sing
> Through every wing;
> And every trumpet through the holy Streets
> As lustre from their chime of pearl repeats.

The published version of the poem still has technical weaknesses and presents uncertainties. But he is hard of heart indeed who can fail to be moved by it.

in youth-time:	Both autographs read *+ youth-time*
Earth:	As in both autographs; MCT loses the capital
women:	As in both autographs; MCT curiously has *woman*, which seems almost certainly to be a printer's error; Sturge Moore also replaces the plural in his SMF text.
Let Faith:	The working draft has a different close to the stanza:

> Let me be taught,
> My Bridegroom, as a child to reach
> Past death the passion Thou would'st teach.

Change:	The fair copy has the initial heavily corrected to a capital, which emphasises that the 'change' is death, as in v8 of the above original draft. The MCT uncorrected version seems gauche unless this allusion is picked up.
Their promise:	Henry obviously had problems with this line; the eventual autograph curiously reads *By promise their first passion stung*, which seems to make little sense.
pass:	In the sense *pass over* (die).

Jusqu'à Demain

Sweet, with my God, I did prevail
That thou with me should'st keep my Feast;
Now, like the Princess in the Arab song,
Who would her life prolong
    With conte on conte increast,
    Yet for another Feast I would make bold—
Lo, Advent followeth hard upon . . .
    So many stars there are,
And yet with her to wake the Morning Star;
    And then, and then,
God will be dying in our midst again . . .
As from the grave He springs,
Lord, shall they be disjointed things
Our alleluias? Put this prayer aside,
And answer it at Whitsuntide.

T1673   Published posthumously in THE WATTLEFOLD, TWF 192, in a subgroup
titled *The Fall of the Leaf*. Emily Fortey's source autograph appears not to
have survived; the printed text bears the footnote *St. Michael's Feast, 1912*.
This is entirely consistent with Henry's Journal entry for that date (they had returned
from Rottingdean the previous day): 'Sweet triumph over Time & space that we are
here & not at Rottingdean for our Archangel's feast— that we light our altars in our
dear Rooms' (ZKC 128a).

Jusqu'à Demain:	Until Tomorrow.
my Feast :	29 September 1912. Michael was known as 'Archangel' at least from the early 1890's (ZCE 100o).
Princess:	Shīrazād, the protagonist of "The Thousand and One Nights" (*Alf laylah wa-laylah*); wife of the murderous sultan Shahriyār, she escaped the fate of his previous quotidian wives by a seemingly inexhaustible repertoire of dawn-stories; each morning she broke off at a tantalising point, just as she was due to be executed.
conte:	Tale. It is possible Michael Field had read the first European translation, a 12 volume *Les Mille et Une Nuits* of Antoine Galland (1704-17), or even the fruitier version by J. C. Mardrus (1899). Sir Richard Burton's 16 volume *The Thousand Nights and a Night* (1885-8) is probably the best known English version, and he was surely one of the most suitable people to undertake it.
Advent:	1 December 1912
from the grave:	Easter Sunday was to be 23 March 1913.
Whitsuntide:	11 May 1913. On that day Henry was indeed still alive, and writing in the Journal 'I am much better' (ZKD 44b).

Index of poems in respect to prior publication

Sixty eight of the poems have appeared before in print:

The remaining thirty three are here printed for the first time:

Index of titles and incipits

Basel Hauptbahnhof, March 1978

IVOR C TREBY researched and assembled
The Michael Field Catalogue: a book of lists
(De Blackland Press ISBN 0 907404 03 0)

He is also the author of four collections of poetry.